Praise for PATIENCE AND FORTITUDE

"With cool acuity, Scott Sherman details the insidious threat to one of the world's greatest cultural institutions, and the gritty resistance that saved it. Anyone who cares about the future of books should read *Patience and Fortitude*."

—PANKAJ MISHRA, author of *From the Ruins of Empire*

"The battle over the New York Public Library was such an important fight to win, and Scott Sherman's reporting was an essential part of that victory."

—SALMAN RUSHDIE, author of *Midnight's Children*

"It's very hard to produce a specific, inarguable example of the power of the press—but here's one. Scott Sherman's pathbreaking 2011 article in *The Nation* about the New York Public Library's plans to demolish much of its headquarters building and substantially change its purpose led directly to that misguided plan's being abandoned three years later. Now Sherman lays out the entire story, from conception to cancellation, of the Central Library Plan. It is an absorbing narrative, and more; it also gets to the heart of an urgent broader issue, the danger our most precious institutions face in the age of disruption."

—NICHOLAS LEMANN, author of *The Big Test*

"Scott Sherman's fast-paced story is a nuanced, disturbing account of what happens when the age of hedge funds, metrics, and management consultants meets one of our country's great institutions of learning. *Patience and Fortitude* is all the more fascinating because Sherman's journalism played a significant role in preventing a cultural atrocity."

—ADAM HOCHSCHILD, author of *King Leopold's Ghost*

"One can read Scott Sherman's engrossing book as a critique of the New York Public Library's stumbles, or as a love letter to a priceless institution. This is a love letter, and one that assails those the author believes would have violated the Library's legacy. Even those who disagree with Sherman should tip their hats to him, for his passion and rigorous reporting, as this book reveals, has aided a great and priceless institution."

—KEN AULETTA, author of *Googled*

"When civic vandals masquerading as visionaries attempted to gut the New York Public Library, Scott Sherman's intrepid reporting in *The Nation* shut them down. Now he gives us the full story, a riveting activist adventure yarn written with the elegance of a cultural romantic and the gimlet eye of an investigative journalist. What I learned is that a civilization traduces its libraries—especially this Library—at its peril."

—RICK PERLSTEIN, author of *The Invisible Bridge*

"With reportorial doggedness, narrative élan, and an unfailing eye for the lancing detail, Scott Sherman masterfully tells the story, by turns enraging and heartening, of the plight of New York's most storied institution in an uncertain age." —TOM VANDERBILT, author of *Traffic*

"Scott Sherman's *Patience and Fortitude* is a gripping, meticulously reported account of the plan to gut a world-famous research library—and the movement that sprung up to preserve it. Like Nicholson Baker's *Double Fold*, another provocative story about a debacle in the stacks, this riveting book shows just how bloody the fight over our cultural treasures can get."

—MARILYN JOHNSON, author of *This Book Is Overdue!*

PATIENCE
AND
FORTITUDE

SCOTT SHERMAN

PATIENCE AND FORTITUDE

POWER, REAL ESTATE, AND THE FIGHT TO SAVE A PUBLIC LIBRARY

MELVILLE HOUSE
BROOKLYN • LONDON

PATIENCE AND FORTITUDE

First Melville House Printing: June 2015

Grateful acknowledgment is made to Brandon Stanton for permission to reprint his photograph on page 160, and to Art Spiegelman for permission to reprint his art on page 162.

Portions of this book originally appeared, in substantially different form, in *The Nation*

Melville House Publishing
46 John Street
Brooklyn, NY 11201

and

8 Blackstock Mews
Islington
London N4 2BT

mhpbooks.com facebook.com/mhpbooks @melvillehouse

Library of Congress Cataloging-in-Publication Data
Sherman, Scott (Scott G.)
Patience and fortitude : power, real estate, and the fight to save a public library / Scott Sherman.
pages cm
ISBN 978-1-61219-429-5 (hardback)
ISBN 978-1-61219-430-1 (ebook)
1. New York Public Library—History. 2. New York Public Library—Administration. 3. New York Public Library—Finance. 4. New York Public Library—Buildings. 5. New York Public Library—Public opinion. 6. Stephen A. Schwarzman Building (New York, N.Y.)—Public opinion. 7. Public opinion—New York (State)—New York. 8. Library buildings—Remodeling—New York (State)—New York. 9. Historic preservation—New York (State)—New York—Citizen participation. 10. New York (N.Y.)—Politics and government—1951- I. Title.
Z733.N6S54 2015
027.4747—dc23

2015013284

Printed in the United States of America
10 9 8 7 6 5 4 3 2 1

With thanks to the Furthermore grants in publishing, a program of the J. M. Kaplan Fund.

TO BHARATI SADASIVAM

"My library was dukedom large enough."

—Shakespeare, *The Tempest*

CONTENTS

PREFACE:
"THERE WILL NEVER BE AN END TO THIS LIBRARY"

This is a book about a world-class library that lost its way in the digital age.

In the late spring of 2011, Katrina vanden Heuvel, editor and publisher of *The Nation*, asked if I might be interested in writing a profile of Anthony Marx, the Amherst College president who had recently agreed to lead the New York Public Library (NYPL). "Lots of unhappy rumblings about how oligarchs"—on the Library's board of trustees—"are taking over too much of a major cultural institution as it celebrates its centennial," vanden Heuvel wrote. She envisioned a story about a "clash of civilizations at the outpost of civilization."

The New York Public Library was an institution that mattered to me personally: as a writer, I had depended on the grand building on 42nd Street for twenty years, and had come to see how fully it embodied its nickname: "the people's library."

It was a place for both Shakespeare scholars and shoeshine boys. When the building turned seventy-five in 1986, Senator Daniel Patrick Moynihan, who had toiled as a bootblack in Times Square in the 1940s, recalled: "It was the first time I was taught that I was welcome in a place of education and learning. I would go into that great marble palace, and I would check my shoeshine box. A gentleman in a brown cotton jacket would take it as if I'd passed over an umbrella and a bowler hat."

I accepted the assignment, and soon reached out to a prominent academic librarian. Halfway through our conversation, he mentioned—rather casually—that the NYPL would soon remove the entire collection of books from the iron-and-steel stacks inside the 42nd Street building and send them to an offsite storage facility in Princeton, New Jersey. This was troubling news: the stacks' three million books were the heart of the institution.

When I asked about this project, NYPL officials confirmed their intentions: the books would leave the building as part of a "Central Library Plan" (CLP), a wide-ranging reconfiguration of services, and the stacks would indeed be demolished. The CLP had been born in June 2007 and was announced to the public nine months later at a little-noticed press conference featuring the novelist (and NYPL trustee) Toni Morrison, who called the plan "truly astonishing." The CLP aimed to consolidate three Midtown libraries into one colossal circulating library inside the 42nd Street building, which would undergo a $300 million renovation by Norman Foster, the British architect. (Frank Gehry had been on the shortlist for the job.)

The project was derailed by the recession of 2008. Fortuitously, I began my reporting as it was quietly being revived. My story, which appeared in *The Nation* in December 2011 under the headline "Upheaval at The New York Public Library," launched a controversy that raged for two and a half years and resulted in more than forty stories in *The New York Times* alone. The debate accelerated in December 2012 when Ada Louise Huxtable, the eminent ninety-one-year-old architecture critic, excoriated the project in the pages of *The Wall Street Journal*; it continued to escalate after her death a few weeks later. The dispute would eventually draw in a cast that included Tom Stoppard, Gloria Steinem, Susan Sarandon, Garrison Keillor, Salman Rushdie, Malcolm Gladwell, Donna Tartt, Art Spiegelman, and the Rev. Al Sharpton. The wrangle over the Central Library Plan, wrote *Publishers Weekly*, amounted to "the biggest public outcry a public library project has ever generated."

The battle to save the NYPL was conducted by a small group of writers, professors, independent scholars, and historic preservationists, who viewed the institution as a sacred public trust. For these critics, the CLP was nothing more than a set of tawdry real-estate deals, a desecration of a historic building, and a betrayal of the NYPL's founding mission. In the words of a leading activist, the historian Joan

Scott, the campaign was about "saving a major institution for the public good."

On the other side were the Library's trustees, who insisted that the NYPL had to be pruned and modernized for the digital age, when many public libraries have prioritized spaces for community engagement and coffee shops over books and bookshelves. The trustees argued that by "monetizing non-core assets"—that is, selling the NYPL's own real estate—the plan would generate up to $15 million per year in badly needed revenue. For inspiration, the NYPL's leaders did not look to other libraries, but to FedEx, Netflix, and Barnes & Noble; they also put their faith in Google, which was scanning millions of books from research libraries across the nation, including the NYPL. To counter the opposition, Anthony Marx rallied construction unions and Teamsters and accused the critics of "elitism"; their intent, he suggested, was to preserve the 42nd Street Library as an exclusive sanctuary for scholars and intellectuals.

It was a charged battle over books, real estate, and architecture, and about the future of an institution that its former president, Vartan Gregorian, called "a treasured repository of civilization." As Gregorian told *The New Yorker* in 1986:

> Libraries keep the records on behalf of all humanity... endless sources of knowledge are *here*. We have books in three thousand languages and dialects. I can take you through here from Balanchine to Tibet. There are esoterica on synthetic fuels, neglected maps of the

> Falklands which were suddenly in demand at the time of the Falklands War. And Warsaw telephone directories from the years of the Holocaust, often invaluable as the only source of documentation of who lived where, in order to substantiate claims for retribution. There will never be an end to this library. Never!

In the 1890s, a group of wealthy men—bankers, corporate titans, philanthropists—came together to create the New York Public Library. These men were cautious individuals with a sense of proportion, who understood the fragility of the institution they had built. Over a century later, the CLP became a project closely tied to another wealthy man: the billionaire Mayor Michael Bloomberg, whose personal friends and family members initiated it. Unlike their late nineteenth-century predecessors, these individuals lacked prudence: they applied radical, free-market solutions to complex institutional problems. In the end, elected officials in New York City had to save the NYPL from its own trustees.

PATIENCE AND FORTITUDE

1

"A Great Work"

"It was Tim Costello who told me to get out of his bar and walk a few blocks to where I'd see two lions, and to go in there and get myself a library card," the writer Frank McCourt recalled in 1997. It was the early 1950s, and McCourt had just arrived in New York from Limerick, Ireland. He entered the building at 42nd Street and climbed the marble staircase. "Up on the third floor, I discovered Paradise: the great reference room with its hundreds of index-card drawers. I asked a librarian if it would be all right to look in the drawers and he said, 'Of course, of course, anything you like.'"

In a 1956 essay, Meyer Berger, a celebrated columnist for *The New York Times*, called the 42nd Street Library "a romantic and mysterious place beyond musty routine." For me, a freelance journalist for years, the romance and mystery are most palpable at 10 a.m., when the building opens its doors. At that hour, sunbeams stream through the tall windows of the Rose Reading Room, glazing the long wooden tables. Chairs lightly scrape the floor; librarians murmur to one another; serenity prevails. In his memoirs, Henry Miller recalled the "good feeling" of working here, in a room "the size of a cathedral, under a lofty ceiling which was an imitation of heaven itself."

Before long, this place will be full—mainly with tourists taking pictures, but also with historians chasing sources, students studying for the LSAT, fact-checkers poring over galleys of magazine articles, people doing crossword puzzles, elderly men dozing. But at this early hour the room contains only a few individuals: a graduate student in a black miniskirt lost in a book by Roland Barthes; an African American gentleman in a suit, his hair streaked with gray, hunched over a bulky volume containing the *Proceedings* of the Jamaican legislature; a young man with a shaggy beard, tapping away at his phone, his guitar case leaning against the table. In frenetic Manhattan, this is an incomparable sanctuary.

Sitting at one of the long wooden tables, I sometimes think about the geniuses and luminaries who toiled in this building. After he arrived in Greenwich Village, but before he began to write his own songs, Bob Dylan came here to read nineteenth-century newspapers on microfilm. "I couldn't exactly put in words what I was looking for," Dylan wrote in *Chronicles: Volume One*, "but I began searching in principle for it, over at the New York Public Library . . . a building that radiates triumph and glory when you walk inside." On those reels containing old editions of *The Savannah Daily Herald*, *The Pennsylvania Freeman*, and *The Brooklyn Daily Times*, Dylan encountered the raw material that would fuel his imagination—news items about "reform movements, anti-gambling leagues, rising crime, child labor, temperance, slave-wage factories, loyalty oaths and religious revivals," as well as stories about William Lloyd Garrison and Abraham Lincoln.

In the NYPL's Allen Room, Betty Friedan composed *The Feminine Mystique* and Robert Caro wrote *The Power Broker*. The list of notable people who have used the 42nd Street building over the years would be nearly impossible to compose, but it would surely include, among many others, Leon Trotsky, Bertolt Brecht, Willa Cather, Francis Ford Coppola, Jacqueline Onassis, Grace Kelly, Marlene Dietrich, Vladimir Nabokov, Joseph Mitchell, Pete Seeger, Isaac Bashevis Singer, Arthur Miller, Norman Mailer, Lou Reed, Philip Roth, Oliver Sacks, Joan Didion, Orhan Pamuk, and Stephen Colbert.

The NYPL's librarians have a predilection for scrutinizing the names on the paper call slips. In the mid-1980s, a staff member, Bob Dumont, noticed that Mario Vargas Llosa, the Peruvian novelist, was seated at one of the long wooden tables, lost in a marathon bout of reading. Dumont admired Vargas Llosa's novels and wanted to chat, but he gave the writer his privacy.

Many years later, in 2008, Dumont again saw Vargas Llosa at one of the long tables; he was researching the life of Roger Casement, the Irish nationalist patriot and human rights activist hanged by the British in 1916. Dumont started a conversation, which they soon continued at an Irish pub around the corner. The librarian then arranged for Vargas Llosa to visit the NYPL's Berg Collection, where he was shown a writing pen that belonged to Dickens; a portable writing desk used by one of the Brontë sisters; a typescript of Conrad's *Heart of Darkness*; Virginia Woolf's diaries; and a rare photograph of Jorge Luis Borges. Vargas Llosa, who received the Nobel Prize in literature in 2010, would repay his debt to the NYPL: when the controversy over the Central Library Plan erupted in early 2012, he was the first major writer to sign a petition opposing the Library's decision to demolish its historic book stacks and sell its real estate.

Of course, most NYPL users have toiled in obscurity. In his essay, Berger described a graduate student from Harvard who was busy with a monumental project in the Library's basement. His task was to read and organize the voluminous archive of Moses Taylor, a nineteenth-century merchant and founder of the City Bank of New York (which evolved into today's Citigroup), whose papers were discovered in sixty-three chests in a warehouse on the New York waterfront. The tale, as told by Berger, appears fanciful, but it is true:

> By the end of 1954, the Harvard man had spent three years in the basement, working on the project without pay. He became one of the palace's most mysterious figures, a tall, handsome fellow who moved below street level among brooding shadows, with a white

> and crimson bathrobe over his street clothes, wearing a miner's mask to filter out the heavy brown dust that spurts from old papers. The Manuscript people are grateful for his labor of love. They said, "We couldn't have done it for years to come and it would have cost easily between $6,000 and $10,000."

Later, in a book, Berger revealed the student's name, Roland Taylor Ely, and offered additional details about his exertions underground: "Few know his identity or his purpose even now. He smiles easily, though. He likes to tell how he fought boredom in the cellar one day, rigging a Boy Scout trap of cardboard to catch a mouse, which he let go." Ely is gone, but the Moses Taylor Papers remain in the depths of the 42nd Street Library: 326 boxes, 132 linear feet, call number MssCol2955.

Despite its name, the New York Public Library is a private nonprofit organization, not a government agency. It was born in 1895 from the consolidation of two nineteenth-century libraries owned by wealthy men: merchant John Jacob Astor and philanthropist-collector James Lenox. The Astor Library building (which is now the Public Theater, on the edge of the East Village) contained 260,000 volumes in history, literature, science, and art; its users included Nathaniel Hawthorne. The Lenox Library (which occupied the site of what is today the Frick Collection) specialized in

Milton, Shakespeare, and Bunyan. By the 1890s, both libraries faced a shortage of funds, and a far-sighted decision was made: using $2.4 million from the estate of former governor Samuel Tilden, the two would be merged into one central library, in the heart of bustling Manhattan—a library that, its founders hoped, would rival the British Museum and the Bibliothèque nationale in Paris.

New York Mayor Robert Van Wyck, a creature of Tammany Hall, at first resisted the creation of the NYPL. But newspapers, notably Joseph Pulitzer's *New York World*, initiated a crusade to bring it to fruition. When the mayor changed course, the *World* wrote: "The idea that . . . a public library was for a small class of rich men and bookworms has been destroyed."

A library in Manhattan on the scale of the British Museum, built on the site of the old Croton Reservoir, would be a massive undertaking; the trustees needed a visionary to carry it out. They found one: Dr. John Shaw Billings. Phyllis Dain, in her 1972 history of the NYPL, referred to Billings as "probably the most versatile librarian that the United States has produced." He was also one of the most outstanding physicians of his era, a polymath whose interests included hospital construction, sanitary engineering, and medical bibliography.

Raised in rural Indiana, Billings, who had piercing blue eyes and a walrus mustache, served as an army surgeon during the Civil War, during which he performed more than five hundred leg amputations; he also saw duty at the Battle of Gettsyburg. In 1864, he led an expedition to one of Haiti's satellite islands to rescue freed slaves who were stranded in an ill-fated colonization scheme. Dain called him "a man of the world and in the world," one who "inspired affection as well as obedience in those who worked for him."

It was Billings who conceived and designed the new library at 42nd Street, the top floor of which would have a colossal, tranquil, sunlit reading room, built above seven levels of elaborately constructed book stacks. Billings and his collaborator, William Ware, the founder of Columbia University's School of Architecture, wanted books and readers in close proximity.

Six architects, including the preeminent firm of the day, McKim, Mead & White, were on the shortlist, but the trustees selected the little-known John Merven Carrère and Thomas Hastings, whose proposal was celebrated in the press: "Hail to The New York Public Library!" declared a *New York Herald* article, which predicted that the building "will be a marvel of architectural grandeur."

Work began in 1899; the cornerstone was laid in 1902. Labor militancy impeded progress, but the building was finally completed in 1911. It was designed according to the classical principles of the École des Beaux-Arts in Paris, where the architects were trained. Carrère and Hastings insisted on ornately carved ceilings and doors, as well as variegated marble and tile floors; the two architects oversaw the design of the furniture and the custom-made fittings.

In his 1923 book on the NYPL, Harry Lydenberg, a senior

Library official, provided a fine-grained account of the building's interior: "The Current Periodical Room is finished in French walnut . . . Philippine teak is used for the floor of the trustees room . . . The brownish grey marble [in the Reading Room] is Touraine or Basville marble from France."

The lions guarding the Fifth Avenue entrance were designed by the sculptor Edward C. Potter. In the 1930s, Mayor Fiorello La Guardia named them Patience and Fortitude—virtues, he felt, that city residents needed to endure the Depression.

The final cost was $9 million, an enormous sum for 1911; even the Library of Congress had been built for less. Ten workmen lost their lives during the construction; twenty others sustained serious injuries. Carrère himself did not live to see the completion of his masterwork: on March 1, 1911, a Manhattan streetcar collided with his taxicab. The NYPL's trustees opened the building, for the first time, to allow his body to lie in state in the rotunda. Six colleagues from Carrère's firm carried the coffin, which was covered with lilies, and two thousand people viewed it during the hour it was displayed. Thomas Hastings lived until 1929.

President William Howard Taft inaugurated the Library on May 23, 1911. When the doors opened the next day, at least 30,000 people streamed inside. The first book requested was Delia Bacon's *The Philosophy of the Plays of Shakespeare Unfolded*, which the new Library didn't own. The second request was delivered seven minutes after the call slip was submitted: the book was a Russian-language study of Nietzsche and Tolstoy, and the reader was David Shub, a Russian émigré.

Ecstatic commentary about the Library flooded the newspapers. But there was carping, too, from architecture critics. "Although regarded as important and distinguished," Dain wrote, "the new library did not win recognition as a totally beautiful building like the Boston Public Library." But its eminence has grown over time. Writing in *The New Criterion* in 2013, Michael J. Lewis, an architectural historian at Williams College, noted that the 42nd Street Library "is America's finest classical revival building, and it is also our greatest civic building."

Carrère and Hastings also designed a number of the NYPL branch (or neighborhood) libraries, including one in the Hunts Point section of the Bronx, the exterior of which was conceived in "14th century Florentine style." Credit for that branch, and many others, can be traced to the industrialist Andrew Carnegie who, in 1901, pledged $5.2 million for the creation of sixty-five branch libraries in New York City. (He had a national commitment to libraries, building 1,700 of them across the country.) Libraries fit neatly into Carnegie's bootstrap philosophy. "The fundamental advantage of a library is that it gives nothing for nothing," he declared. "Youths must acquire knowledge themselves."

The city's newspapers rejoiced over the gift. The *World* highlighted New York City's feeble commitment to its public libraries, which amounted to nine cents per capita, compared to fifty cents in Boston, forty-one cents in Buffalo, and fifteen cents in Chicago. Not everyone lauded Carnegie, however: Upton Sinclair penned a satirical poem about the industrialist, and Mark Twain accused him of vanity. The problem, it turned out, wasn't his vanity, but the terms of his gift: Carnegie built the libraries, but entrusted their financing and upkeep to local politicians, who, in subsequent decades, would not always take that responsibility seriously.

Still, Carnegie's action had deep, lasting results. In 1901, the city possessed a variety of circulating libraries, some of which were located in the slums of the Lower East Side; others were under the control of the Catholic Archdiocese. Carnegie's gift spurred politicians to absorb those libraries into a unified NYPL system that contained both the neighborhood libraries and the monumental structure that was rising at 42nd Street.

The branch libraries, many of which were built with stone fronts, classical columns, and arched windows and doors, were immensely popular, and were administered by enlightened individuals. Though the 42nd Street building was the star of the system, managers took great care to ensure the vitality of the branches. First-rate consultants assisted with the selection of materials: John Dewey, for instance, helped to choose philosophy titles for the neighborhood libraries, some of whose walls contained paintings on loan from the Metropolitan Museum of Art.

In a city of immigrants, the branch libraries formed a

sturdy ladder to the middle class. Civil service employees and teachers found them a congenial place to study for promotional exams; newcomers to the United States flocked to them for books in dozens of languages. The NYPL's Traveling Library Office delivered books to factories, fire stations, hospitals, mental hospitals, prisons, newsboys' clubs, and longshoremen and sailors' reading rooms. More than a million books were delivered by that department in 1910 alone.

The NYPL also blazed a path in children's services. In 1906, the Library hired a dynamic thirty-five-year-old woman, Annie Moore, to run the children's services department, and in her first year on the job she demanded (and received) a $10,000 increase in her book budget; she also lifted the age restrictions for children in NYPL facilities, a bold reform for that day and age. Dain wrote that Moore had "an uncompromising insistence on well-written, well-made books" for children.

The nerve center of the NYPL remained the landmark structure built by Carrère and Hastings, which, despite its imposing grandeur, quickly became known as a library for the masses. Memoirs by NYPL staff members convey an atmosphere, in the 1920s and '30s, of intellectual devotion and moralism at 42nd Street. In his quirky book *Random Recollections of an Anachronism: or Seventy-Five Years of Library Work* (1980), Keyes DeWitt Metcalf, a senior NYPL administrator, noted that between 1919 and 1937 he experienced only two minor flare-ups with his boss, Harry Lydenberg, who administered the 42nd Street Library. "The first was when I had missed the review of an important work on anthropology in the *London Times Literary Supplement*. Instead of rebuking me, he quietly asked me how in the world it had happened."

In those years, the Library kept its most sensitive documents—material about sex and atheistic pamphlets assailing the Bible—in a special "cage" surrounded by heavy wire grating on the sixth floor of the book stacks underneath the Main Reading Room. Only two staff members—Mr. Metcalf being one of them—had keys to the "cage." One morning Mr. Metcalf noticed with concern that a book from the "cage" was missing: a poem by a distinguished American author, an "item for which a considerable number of men who made collections of erotica were ready to pay a large sum." He suspected that the thief was one of the unruly "stack boys" whose job was to retrieve material from the vast storage space in the heart of the building.

That very afternoon, returning home on the subway, Metcalf noticed that a young man seated next to him was holding the purloined book. The librarian followed him off the train and accosted him on the street. "I told him I had seen him reading the stolen book and that I was going home with him to see what else he had there":

> He took me through the house, including his own room. There were practically no books or papers to be

> found. He convinced me that this was his first offense. He told me that he had obtained the book by taking a rod from the shelf-list drawer and pushing the volume under the grating on to the stack aisle floor, and then with a broom handle taken from the janitor's closet he had been able to push it along and work it out under the door into the main stack aisle. The book was thin and was easy to push under the door. I told him not to come back to the library and that the case would not be taken to court.

In the early decades of the NYPL, the trustees were determined to fashion a collection that would rank among the world's finest. Librarians had wide latitude to purchase materials. In 1929, a professor from the University of Chicago went to Europe and surveyed social scientists about the most essential books published for research libraries that year in England, France, and Germany. Metcalf, in his memoirs, quietly acknowledged the results: "The Library of Congress and Harvard had 60 to 62 percent" of the books; "but the New York Public Library . . . had 92 percent."

The Library also received a multitude of items from donors, some of which began to arrive even before the 42nd Street building was completed. In 1899, the NYPL obtained a cache of books and pamphlets on Mormonism—451 volumes, 325 pamphlets, and 52 volumes of newspapers. The letter of presentation, from Helen Miller Gould (Jay Gould's daughter), began:

> Dear Sir:—
>
> It gives me pleasure to add the Berrian collection of books and pamphlets on Mormonism to the New York Public Library, for I believe it will be very useful for students to have access to a collection that gives a clear idea of this peculiar form of error. The Mormon Elders are proselyting in many sections of our country, and our people generally should become better informed on the subject of Mormonism in order to be on their guard against these "Latter Day Saints" as they style themselves. Hoping that the books will prove useful . . .

In 1900, the Library received a remarkable art collection from Samuel P. Avery, which contained 17,557 items, among them etchings by James McNeill Whistler, Jean-François Millet, and Charles-François Daubigny, as well as J.M.W. Turner's *Liber Studiorum*, a series of landscape and seascape compositions. In 1907, 239 letters by Karl Marx and Friedrich Engels entered the collection. Not long after that, 1,600 volumes and pamphlets on meteorology and terrestrial magnetism collected at the Central Park Observatory found their way to 42nd Street.

A benefactor of the NYPL perished on the *Titanic*. William Spencer, an American citizen who lived in Paris, bequeathed to the NYPL, along with a substantial sum of money, 232 illustrated books with ornate bindings, some of which had taken two years to execute. These volumes constitute the core of the Library's Spencer Collection, the finest materials of which were sent to offsite storage the day after Pearl Harbor was attacked.

In their quest for international distinction, the Library's trustees frequented the auction houses. Writing in the left-wing *New Masses* in 1939, a skeptic wondered why in 1932, in the depths of the Depression, "when the book stock was being rapidly depleted," the NYPL's trustees paid $68,000 for a rare fourteenth-century English manuscript, the *Tickhill Psalter*. Yet there were always limitations as to what the NYPL could purchase: in 1939, the Library declined the papers of Franz Kafka; tight finances prevented that acquisition. Then, as now, there was tension between the needs of the branch libraries and the requirements and ambitions of the research division.

A multitude of white faces filled the 42nd Street building in the first decades of its existence; the first black librarian was hired only in 1945. How did black New Yorkers view the NYPL? A clue can be found in James Baldwin's first novel, *Go Tell It on the Mountain* (1953), in which a boy from Harlem gazes at the majestic marble structure:

> A building filled with books and unimaginably vast, and which he had never yet dared to enter . . . he had never gone in because the building was so big that it must be full of corridors and marble steps, in the maze

> of which he would be lost and never find the book he wanted. And then everyone, all the white people inside, would know that he was not used to great buildings, or to many books, and they would look at him with pity.

The NYPL was beginning to amass a deep archive of materials pertaining to black history and culture. Much credit for this belongs to Arthur Alfonso Schomburg (1874–1938), a Puerto Rican–born bibliophile. Documenting the black experience was his life's work: during one expedition to second-hand bookshops in the 1930s, Schomburg, according to his biographer Elinor des Verney Sinnette, purchased ten different editions of *Uncle Tom's Cabin* for twenty-five cents each. In his personal archive were letters by Frederick Douglass and Booker T. Washington; army orders signed by the Haitian revolutionary Toussaint L'Ouverture; and certificates of slave sales. Schomburg was not wealthy, so friends gave him books: Langston Hughes sent him volumes about Pushkin.

In 1926, the Carnegie Corporation, endowed by the industrialist, purchased Schomburg's entire collection for $10,000 and donated it to the 135th Street branch of the NYPL: the Schomburg Collection was born, and it became a sanctuary for writers, activists, intellectuals, students, and the citizenry at large. In 1938, when the young Ralph Ellison was doing research for the Works Progress Administration, he spent countless hours at the Schomburg and found the collection "a revelation," according to his biographer, Arnold Rampersad.

Kenneth B. Clark, the psychologist and civil rights activist, has recalled his first visit to the Schomburg at the age of twelve. He was a bookish Harlem boy in pursuit of cerebral adventures, which led him "upstairs to the third floor to that forbidden and mysterious area reserved for adults." Schomburg rose from his desk to greet him; they sat and talked about black luminaries—"men like Ira Aldridge in his role as Othello." The boy became one of those luminaries: in 1954, when the Supreme Court issued its ruling on *Brown v. Board of Education*, it cited research material on school segregation that Clark had gathered at the Schomburg Library.

Despite lean budgets and paltry resources, the Schomburg would later acquire invaluable material pertaining to Harriet Tubman, Richard Wright, Langston Hughes, Paul Robeson, Zora Neale Hurston, Nat King Cole, Fats Waller, Josephine Baker, Romare Bearden, Amiri Baraka, and Arthur Ashe. Its holdings include the Brotherhood of Sleeping Car Porters Collection; the 1964 Mississippi Freedom Summer Project Collection; the Biafra War Collection; and the FBI files on the Black Panther Party.

The Schomburg Library, always a beacon for Harlem and the black diaspora, wasn't just a place for scholarly contemplation: the American Negro Theater staged plays in the basement, in which the young Sidney Poitier and Harry Belafonte appeared.

•

The NYPL reached its apogee in the 1940s and '50s. The Library's annual reports from the early 1940s are proof of its professionalism and sense of purpose: they are book-length documents written with flair, and alive with vivid bibliographical details about the research collection; never again would the annual reports reach that level of distinction. The trustees were proud of what they had achieved, and that pride imbued Meyer Berger's 1956 essay, in which he noted that the NYPL had even played a significant role in World War II: "Much of the information that gave Allied commanders a complete picture of the North African and Normandy coasts came from The New York Public Library." Research for the Manhattan Project was undertaken at the Library, and the private sector, too, relied on the NYPL: representatives from *Time* magazine, Metro-Goldwyn-Mayer, IBM, General Electric, and the Chase Manhattan Bank all used the collections, as did an army of small entrepreneurs and investors who haunted the corridors and reading rooms.

In 1961, when the 42nd Street Library turned fifty, the trustees hired William K. Zinsser of *The New York Herald Tribune* to compose an anniversary booklet. Zinsser was struck by the Library's international acquisitions: "The man buying political pamphlets in the outdoor markets of Ghana this week is quite likely to be acting on orders from Fifth Avenue and 42nd Street." The depth and quirkiness of the collections also stirred the NYPL's chronicler, who listed some of his personal favorites: more than a million playbills going back to 1750; the programs of every Broadway play for a century; "route books" for circuses and secret material from the Society of American Magicians, "which may be seen only by its members"; 70,000 musical recordings; manuscripts of a Bach cantata, a Mozart symphony, and a Beethoven violin sonata, as well as a lock of Franz Liszt's hair; the records of Diaghilev's Ballets Russes; and dazzling illuminated scrolls of *The Tale of Genji.*

In the NYPL's essence, Zinsser discerned "the quality of freedom":

> This is a building that takes no sides because it presents all sides. It grants its visitors the dignity of free access to information. It does not hide the ugly or censor the injurious. These guarantees are woven through every division, and often they take extraordinary form. The Jewish Division owns the biggest known mass of anti-Semitic material; the Picture Collection has hundreds of racist cartoons; the Current Periodicals Room subscribes to subversive magazines.

Dr. John Shaw Billings, the polymath and Civil War veteran, deserves much of the credit for the NYPL's singular triumph. Billings battled cancer of the lip and other ailments, and he passed away in 1913, just two years after the 42nd Street building was completed. A few months before his death, Billings received a letter from a dear friend on the Library's board of trustees:

If we must depart, and before many years we must, we have unselfishly, honestly and capably done a great work, & we have done it together. The Trustees and Executive Committee were not necessary to this present success, altho they ably contributed—You were—so my old friend my affectionate good wishes for 1913.

2

Decay and Renewal

In 1789, Joshua Reynolds executed a stirring portrait of Elizabeth Billington, an actress and opera singer whose death in Venice in 1818 was probably the result of a beating. The painting, *Mrs. Billington as St. Cecilia*, had belonged to one of the NYPL's founders. On October 17, 1956, at the Parke-Bernet auction house in Manhattan, the NYPL sold the painting to Lord Beaverbrook, the newspaper baron, for $6,500. The same afternoon, the Library also sold a painting by Thomas Gainsborough, for $20,500; a work by John Constable, for $30,000; and two paintings by J.M.W. Turner, which garnered $56,000 and $47,000, respectively.

A structural weakness at the core of the NYPL made those art sales more or less inevitable. The NYPL was created with a peculiar dual structure: the branch library system, which serves Manhattan, the Bronx, and Staten Island

(Brooklyn and Queens have their own separate library networks), is primarily financed by New York City tax revenues, as Carnegie had stipulated. By contrast, the NYPL's research libraries (including 42nd Street) rely on a precarious mix of private philanthropic funds, an endowment, and city, state, and federal aid that is usually too little for the institution's grand responsibilities and ambitions.

The NYPL's economic foundation is exceedingly fragile, which explains why the research division—which grew to include four separate facilities in Manhattan—has been in fiscal distress almost from the beginning; the branch libraries, too, have been underfunded for much of their history.

In the late 1890s, politicians in New York expressed unease about the structure and governance of the NYPL, which was conceived as a private, nonprofit institution, with a self-perpetuating board of trustees drawn from Manhattan's upper crust. The fears of elected officials nearly aborted the NYPL. In 1898, before work even began on the 42nd Street Library, Mayor Van Wyck announced:

> I would be willing to vote $15,000,000 for a public library that the City would own, but instead we are compelled to give land and $6,000,000 for a public library that private individuals will control. The City, however, must pay all the employees and pay the expense. No public lands would be given over to private control if I had the say . . . It is a sort of auxiliary government by societies.

Those private individuals struggled to sustain it. Two world wars left the NYPL in ruinous financial condition. In 1948, the trustees issued a sober fund-raising pamphlet, addressed to the mayor and "the citizens of New York," which emphasized: "The Library is now faced with the gravest crisis in its history." The pamphlet began: "The Library has been hard hit by inflation . . . Unlike business and industry, hospitals and colleges, it cannot even try to keep abreast of rising costs by increasing its fees or prices. It has none to increase. Its charter directs the Trustees to provide a *free* public service . . . The Library must find additional income." The plea fell on deaf ears.

To read the NYPL's annual reports from the 1960s is to confront an institution in distress. Dispiriting phrases appear: "problems of space"; "complex problems of Library"; "the Library's fiscal crisis"; "mounting fiscal deficits and constraints." In 1967, the trustees sold $1.2 million in endowment securities to meet the previous year's deficit. Faced with a choice between spending endowment funds or reducing acquisitions, the trustees chose to plunder the nest egg: "We will deteriorate the endowment rather than the library," an NYPL executive said. A *New York Times* editorial saluted that decision as "courageous."

There were, however, a handful of success stories at the NYPL in the 1960s. In 1965, officials opened the Library for the Performing Arts at Lincoln Center, which not only had a savvy, skilled staff that included former dancers and actors, but also librarians with specialized degrees in fields such as music. But the principal drama at the NYPL in the 1960s took place in Greenwich Village, at the Jefferson Market Courthouse, known as "Old Jeff."

For decades, "Old Jeff" was a building associated with vice, seediness, and violence: in 1906, Harry K. Thaw was arraigned there for the murder of the architect Stanford White. In the early 1950s, Village residents began to pay attention to the courthouse, which had decayed: they discovered that, with its turrets, gables, and high ceilings, it had been voted one of the nation's ten most beautiful buildings when it opened in 1876. In 1958, locals spearheaded a campaign to transform the courthouse—which the City was eager to demolish—into a public library. The NYPL's trustees initially resisted the idea. But citizen action prevailed, and in 1964 work began to turn the building into the principal NYPL branch library in Greenwich Village.

It was a civic triumph. In September 1964, Ada Louise Huxtable, then the forty-three-year-old architecture critic of *The New York Times*, exulted in an essay: "At a time when New York is considering the passage of landmarks legislation, the saga of Greenwich Village's historic courthouse is a case history of how to go about preserving a building when there isn't any official way to do it." Huxtable congratulated local activists: "It is also a study in organized public interest, dogged persistence, practical sentimentality and civic savvy, or how to make a determined group of citizens an effective force for the achievement of an objective generally considered hopeless."

The Jefferson Market branch, which opened in 1967, prompted NYPL trustees to close the facility around the corner—the seventy-nine-year-old Jackson Square Library, a three-story brownstone at 251 West 13th Street, which was donated by Cornelius Vanderbilt's grandson. In 1967, the NYPL sold that brownstone for $82,500.

But the vibrant city that had nourished the NYPL for decades was eroding. In Saul Bellow's *Mr. Sammler's Planet* (1970), a one-eyed Polish intellectual and Holocaust survivor is caught in the swirling chaos of New York City in the late 1960s. Artur Sammler's wife was butchered by the Nazis, and he lives with his torpid niece in a drab West Side apartment. The 42nd Street Library is part of Mr. Sammler's daily routine: he goes there to read manuscripts by thirteenth-century religious writers, which he devours, with his functioning eye, on a microfilm machine.

One afternoon, after witnessing a theft on his way home from 42nd Street, Mr. Sammler approaches a pay phone on Riverside Drive. "Of course the phone was smashed," he says to himself. "Most outdoor telephones were smashed, crippled. They were urinals, also. New York was getting worse than Naples or Salonika."

The Naples effect was a result of debt, shoddy municipal management, and upheavals in the global economy, all of which prompted Abraham Beame, who served as New York's mayor between 1974 and 1977, to implement drastic measures. Beame's principal weapon was austerity: 47,000 municipal employees were dismissed in New York City in 1975–76.

It was a traumatic decade for the NYPL, far worse than the 1960s. In December 1971, colossal banners covered the elegant façade of the 42nd Street Library: "HELP YOUR LIBRARY TODAY." In those years, the NYPL sought creative ways to fund itself: in 1972, under a tent in Bryant Park, William F. Buckley debated John Kenneth Galbraith before eight hundred guests, each of whom paid $100; the proceeds went to the NYPL. Influential friends hatched schemes to assist the institution: Elia Kazan proposed that the author (and publisher) of each novel that reached the top of the bestseller list should donate $1,000 to the Library for every month the book remained atop the list. Kazan made news by presenting a check for $1,000, but his scheme went nowhere.

The NYPL's fate was fervently debated in the press: in 1972, *The New York Times Book Review* published dueling essays by two champions of the institution: Barbara W. Tuchman, the Pulitzer Prize–winning historian, and James Thomas Flexner, the George Washington biographer. Tuchman's essay opened with a dramatic flourish recalling the destruction of the University Library in Louvain, Belgium, which had a unique collection of medieval manuscripts, by the German army in 1914. The Louvain library was felled by violence; Tuchman contended that her library, at 42nd Street, was being steadily eroded by an incendiary degree of neglect: "A lack of adequate funds, the affliction of those of our institutions that serve no special interest but only civilization."

Tuchman adored the 42nd Street facility, which always proved itself to be a gold mine: "In the course of research stretching over 20 years and extending from the Phoenicians of the Bronze Age to the music of Richard Strauss to Americans in China, I asked for only two books, as I remember, which the Library could not produce. One was in their catalog but could not be located, and both they were able to borrow for me."

The starkest illustration of institutional decline, Tuchman wrote, was the demise of evening and weekend hours, and the erosion of the gargantuan card catalog: "In many cases the upper right hand corner of the cards, which carries the class mark, has been blurred or broken off from overuse and lack of replacement. When the class mark goes, chaos comes." Tuchman's solution to the NYPL's entropy was to emulate the Metropolitan Museum of Art and institute a fee:

> If turnstiles were installed requiring the same fare and using the same token as subways and buses, the public, I think, would accept the principle and get used to the idea of paying... The number of persons who entered the Central Building for whatever reason in the fiscal year 1970–1971, whether to read or look at the exhibits or consult the catalog or out-of-town telephone books or merely come in out of the cold, was 1,818,165. At

> 35 cents a head this works out to $636,375.75, a useful sum. It would almost restore the evening hours.

Tuchman understood that charging a fee was anathema to the NYPL's core principles. Still, she felt that "the wide open door . . . was a policy suited to a freer smaller world and many old, free things cannot be sustained under present pressures." (A few months later, she gave the NYPL a $50,000 challenge grant, which helped the Library raise additional funds from the Mobil Oil Foundation and the Standard Oil Company.)

Flexner's rejoinder to Tuchman stressed the NYPL's centrality to the nation's intellectual life: "At a meeting of the New York State Council on the Arts, it was pointed out that if all other education institutions in the state were destroyed, they could (except museums) be re-created from the New York Public Library. But if the Public Library were destroyed, all other institutions combined could not re-create *it*." Like Tuchman, Flexner was a habitual user of the 42nd Street Library, and he knew its cracks and crevices, and its cast of eccentric characters: "The library has her own real children. There is a man who spends hours every day walking noiselessly through the large rooms: his face is mild; he bothers no one; he has found a home." Flexner loathed the idea of a fee: "Let our people go! Let them go unhindered into this temple of self-education." But he offered no solutions to the Library's fiscal woes.

Meanwhile, the NYPL's trustees brawled with the City: a

confrontation between the Library and Mayor Beame unfolded in 1974, during the latter's first year in office. A feeling of desperation had cornered the NYPL's trustees and primed them for a fight. "A prevailing concern in all the events of the last year," NYPL president Richard Couper wrote in the 1974 annual report, "is the ultimate dire effect of the constant nibble, the eating away at the core of what the institution is all about."

In the fall of 1974, the NYPL announced it would permanently close three of its branch libraries unless City Hall released $500,000 that Library officials insisted they needed to fill sixty staff positions. Since two of the branches threatened with elimination—Jefferson Market in Greenwich Village and Co-op City in the Bronx—were situated in neighborhoods with high levels of political participation, the NYPL's threat was interpreted as a surprisingly reckless and aggressive display of brinkmanship by the trustees.

Mayor Beame was livid: he not only lashed the NYPL for inefficiency, but also accused its trustees of neglecting the branch libraries around the city. A bold maneuver by the NYPL's leadership had backfired. "In the fiscal gloom that hangs over City Hall these days," John Darnton wrote in the *Times* on November 15, 1974, "the New York Public Library was the first institution to engage in the delicate business of 'budget brinkmanship' with the money-minded Mayor Beame. It was also the first to lose."

The NYPL's threat to eliminate three of its own branch libraries had a Keystone Cops quality: the trustees never bothered to build grassroots support for their confrontation with the mayor, and some residents of Co-op City and Greenwich Village were embittered. "The Library used blackmail of a community, selective blackmail," one activist told the *Times*. "If the Library had come to the community, they would have gotten support." The trustees capitulated, and the three branches threatened with eradication, including the splendid "Old Jeff," kept their doors open.

The nadir had arrived. The 1976 annual report appeared on butcher paper, and contained an introductory paragraph written by Brooke Astor—the legendary New York philanthropist and one of the NYPL's essential trustees and benefactors—who pointed out that the Library had saved several thousand dollars by printing the document on the cheapest paper available. (The previous year, the NYPL hadn't printed an annual report at all.)

The branches were bleeding. In June 1975, a reporter for the *Times*, Tom Buckley, visited the once-elegant Hunts Point library. The neighborhood had been Jewish and Irish, but now it was Puerto Rican, and impoverished. "There's nothing in this area, not a damn thing," the branch director said. "The playgrounds are full of junkies. The streets are a battlefield. In a couple of weeks the schools will be closed and this will be all they've got." Buckley noted that the branch was facing another 20 percent cut in its budget; his piece was titled "Dimming a Beacon."

In December 1976, delinquents invaded a branch library in the Bronx, near 181st Street, and spent two days inside, vandalizing its contents (including recordings of speeches by Coretta Scott King) and leaving behind empty liquor bottles and discarded food containers. The police found a note that read: "We are having fun . . . it's Christmas day . . . We don't know how to read."

In its first half-century, the NYPL had provided extremely long hours to users, seven days per week: Library officials took pride in the fact that the working class could access Library facilities at night and on weekends. New York's financial collapse in the 1970s ended that accessibility: in early 1977, the NYPL announced that half of its eighty-three branches would be open for only two days a week. Politicians howled.

The 42nd Street Library, too, was reeling. In May 1977, a collection of rare stamps worth $150,000 was stolen; NYPL officials postulated that the thief had hidden himself in the building when it closed, and walked out the next morning with the precious stamps. On October 11, 1977, a pipe bomb exploded at 4 p.m., causing minor damage to the Library's façade, though no one was injured. In June 1979, author Benita Eisler published a startling op-ed in the *Times*, which began:

> I returned to the building from lunch to find a trail of freshly splashed blood, leading from the 42nd Street entrance to the inquiry desk in the main hall. A

mental patient, out on a pass, had repeatedly stabbed a reading room user in the head and neck; the puddles of blood I saw had spurted from the victim as he was rushed to medical facilities on the ground floor.

The Schomburg was also in distress. It had become extremely popular: the movements for civil rights and Black Power led to a surge in attendance. So when smoke filled its reading room in 1974—the empty tenement next door had been set on fire—there was every reason to panic. Fortunately, there were no serious injuries.

The Harlem collections—which included 45,000 books, 1,400 record albums, and 1,100 reels of microfilm—were in precarious condition, and visitors were shocked by what they saw: "The basement . . . is now a dank, dismal place where rotting newspapers are haphazardly stored," a *Times* reporter wrote. "The third floor storeroom resembles a cluttered attic. Art objects lay exposed on open shelves to humidity, heat and dust. Papers of famous people and the records of organizations stand curling and shredding at the edges in uninventoried file cabinets."

The staff of the NYPL, whose salaries were always low, valiantly persevered throughout the 1970s. In 1972, William Cole, an old-timer in the book trade, produced, for the *Times*, a tribute to the beehive-like information desk at the heart of the 42nd Street building, where, surrounded by nine thousand wooden card trays stuffed with ten million cards, librarians took questions all day long. In free moments, they handled queries sent through the mail. "You will always find one librarian working on a 'snag,'" Cole wrote. "These are extremely tough questions that the librarians look on as challenges. They admit that they don't *always* get their man, but almost always."

All through the dismal 1970s, beleaguered librarians and curators produced exhibitions on an extensive range of subjects, harvesting the Library's rich collections: Dickens in America, Verdi in New York, Oscar Wilde's *The Importance of Being Earnest*, Joseph Conrad's *Victory*, Dutch children's books, Copernicus, Paul Robeson, Manhattan's Yiddish theater district, air pollution, devils and demons, Alexander Pushkin, maps in China, and river exploration in Colorado.

But those efforts couldn't alleviate the gloom or reverse the fiscal decline. "The Library Branches Are Dying" read a stark headline over a *Times* editorial in September 1980. It noted that some branches "are open a mere 12 hours *a week*," and lamented the fact that the new mayor, Ed Koch, had slashed the NYPL's budget by another $500,000. "New York already spends less on libraries—$7.14 per capita—than many large cities, including some, like Cleveland, that are also pinched."

"In 1978 when I first signed on to help the New York Public Library, it had almost no reputation left to protect." So wrote former NYPL board chairman Andrew Heiskell in his 1998 memoirs. "The library had no political clout. It had no constituency except scholars, children, and ordinary citizens who like to read." In those years, Heiskell wondered if the NYPL would even survive: "If it had not been for Brooke Astor's mammoth gift of $5 million several years earlier, the Library would have slipped over the edge. Even after her gift, the Library was broke."

In 1981, the trustees initiated a search for a new president. "We needed a charismatic character," one trustee later recalled. Someone recommended the provost of the University of Pennsylvania, Vartan Gregorian—"a funny looking man," in Heiskell's words, "small and stocky with bushy gray-black hair and a strong Armenian accent." In a two-part profile of Gregorian that appeared in *The New Yorker* in 1986, Philip Hamburger observed: "I was immediately struck by his benign resemblance to the two sculptured lions, Patience and Fortitude, that guard the main steps to the library."

At first, Gregorian wasn't sure he wanted the job: he glanced at the 42nd Street facility and saw that the marble was brown with filth, the chandeliers and lighting fixtures contained only two or three bulbs, and the Celeste Bartos Forum, a stately room on the ground floor, had become a storage locker. That very year, in *The New York Review of Books*, Elizabeth Hardwick had written that the 42nd Street Library "has the smell of a tomb." As for the eighty or so branch libraries: they were, in Gregorian's words, "dark, dirty and unsafe."

But he saw the NYPL presidency as a win-win proposition: in his memoir, *The Road to Home* (2003), Gregorian wrote: "If I succeeded in rescuing and rejuvenating the Library and restoring its central role in the cultural and educational life of New York, it would be considered a 'miracle.' If I failed, it would be a worthy yet public 'martyrdom.'"

Born in Tabriz, Iran, and fluent in seven languages, Gregorian is an unusually cosmopolitan figure—an energetic and voluble man, and a genuine humanist and intellectual. A creature of academia, he was a stranger in a strange land: the behavioral patterns and codes of Manhattan society, whose members filled the NYPL's board of trustees, were alien to him. But he was a quick study.

In December 1981, Brooke Astor hosted a dinner for the NYPL's new president at her Park Avenue apartment, aiming to introduce him to the crème de la crème of her circle: the guests included Barbara Walters, Nancy Kissinger, and Oscar de la Renta, as well as Connecticut senator Abraham Ribicoff; Sir John Pope-Hennessy, the curator of the Department of European Paintings at the Metropolitan Museum; and Sir Fitzroy McLean, a World War II hero and an authority on Tito and the Balkans. For Gregorian, whose grandfather had run a caravansary for mules and donkeys and whose mother had died of pneumonia in 1941 at the age of twenty-six, the evening was an "unreal" experience:

> The library was lined on three walls with handsomely bound editions of classic English, French and Russian literature . . . The library and living room were

> decorated with rare drawings and nineteenth- and twentieth-century European paintings, and mementos and gifts from all over the world . . . The cocktail napkins and shiny silver matchboxes bore the initials of Vincent Astor. Waiters served on nineteenth-century fine china with crystal glasses. Mrs. Astor looked splendid in her black velvet dress and her emerald necklace and earrings.

In his eight years at the helm of the NYPL, Gregorian put in long hours, inspired his staff, energized donors, and reminded city leaders of the Library's importance. He was supremely articulate: he transformed the gloomy public discourse around the Library, and invested it with the loftiest values: a decrepit institution was now the embodiment of civilization. "We mirror the world, in all its folly and wisdom," he told *The New Yorker*. "We serve the masses and the individual."

His success wasn't only rhetorical: the endowment reached $172 million, City funding for the research libraries jumped 200 percent, a temperature/humidity control system was installed in the 42nd Street stacks, and a vast storage facility for books was constructed underneath Bryant Park. (The neighborhood got better, too: the renewal of that park meant that the west terrace of the Library would no longer serve as a shooting gallery and public latrine.)

Gregorian had an indispensable partner: Brooke Astor, who became a friend. He valued her aphorisms. On the secret of longevity, she told him: "Be an optimist, be curious, read every night, don't meet the same people all the time, don't be a cynic." He also appreciated her sense of humor: "She told me a journalist once asked her whether she was a lesbian. No, my dear, I am an Episcopalian, she replied." Their friendship yielded concrete benefits for the Library: after much subtle diplomacy, Gregorian eventually persuaded her to give $10 million, an immense sum in the 1980s. (Astor died in 2007 at age 105.)

By 1988, Gregorian was ready to go. "We had succeeded," he proclaimed in his memoirs, "in rescuing the New York Public Library." Without question, the institution he left behind was stronger than the one he had inherited. Still, for all his success, Gregorian couldn't overcome the structural dilemmas that bedeviled the NYPL: federal and state funds for the research division were still limited, and financial support from the City for the sprawling, decrepit branch system was still unreliable.

Eighteen months after Gregorian left, Bruce Weber, a *Times* reporter, went to the Hunts Point branch in the Bronx and was taken to the reading room on the second floor. First he saw that the roof was leaking; then he noticed a strange contraption: "The building's 'intercom' system—a coffee can filled with washers, suspended on a rope, that is rattled to call employees to the phone." Chairman Heiskell told Weber, in an unintended commentary on the Gregorian era: "We can arm wrestle a bit with City Hall, but we're broke."

The perennial search for funding in the years after

Gregorian's departure would lead the NYPL's trustees back to the Library's art collection for the first time since 1956.

On October 15, 2004, a committee of NYPL trustees circulated a fifty-page report stamped "CONFIDENTIAL." Members of the committee included President Paul LeClerc; Robert Darnton, a prominent historian; Neil Rudenstine, a former president of Harvard; two corporate lawyers; an executive of Goldman Sachs; and the art collector Barbara G. Fleischman. The report, written by Rudenstine, would determine the fate of the NYPL's small but very distinguished collection, which contained works by Asher B. Durand, Gilbert Stuart, John Singleton Copley, and Rembrandt Peale.

In those years, prices were soaring in the art world, and many cultural institutions were hastening to "deaccession" their works—i.e., sell them for cash. In 2004, the Field Museum of Natural History in Chicago auctioned works by George Catlin, renowned for his humanistic chronicles of Native Americans in the nineteenth century. One trustee, Edward Hirschland, resigned in protest, arguing, in an interview with the *Chicago Tribune*, that the Catlin Collection wasn't the museum's to sell—it "belong[ed] to the city of Chicago." Hirschland excoriated the logic employed by his fellow trustees: "They call it 'monetizing a non-performing asset.'"

This was the backdrop to the sale of the NYPL's art collection. "The Research Libraries' total budget is under severe pressure," the confidential report began, "and the acquisition budget . . . is in danger of falling seriously behind its historical—and leadership—level." What followed, in language reminiscent of the 1948 fund-raising pamphlet, was a grim recitation of the NYPL's situation vis-à-vis other world-class cultural institutions: "While nearly all not-for-profit educational and cultural institutions—whether they are colleges, symphony orchestras, regional theaters, or museums—frequently face budgetary difficulties, most (not all) of them have several revenue streams that can often balance one another." But the NYPL had few revenue streams:

> By contrast, free-standing libraries—and especially those very few institutions that function as major research libraries of international reputation—face an altogether different set of realities. They do not charge admission or tuition. They mount superb scholarly (and more general) exhibitions, but these are invariably free of charge. They are not likely to have profitable shops, restaurants or parking garages.

The report went on: the NYPL "finds itself in a highly unusual if not unique predicament. Of the greatest libraries in the world, the NYPL is the only private library . . . Indeed, it is difficult to think of a precise analogue to The New York Public Library: that is, an incontestably major international research library—collecting materials in a multitude of fields—that currently must find about 70% of its revenues from the private sector."

The trustees knew that the sale of art could "alienate important donors—and potential future donors—who may be reluctant to give collections to the Library for fear that the materials could in the future be sold." Moreover:

> Selling any major paintings may lead to a very serious split in the Library and its associated communities—staff, friends, users or even members of the city and state government. The action could be divisive, no matter how well it may seem to be justified . . . The media may emphasize all and any differences of opinion, and may criticize the Library . . . Would the dissension and negative publicity be worth the monetary gain even if the proceeds were absolutely restricted in order to strengthen the Library's essential mission?

The trustees believed it was a risk worth taking, and they voted to sell the paintings.

This was a reversal of NYPL policy in the 1980s. When Gregorian first arrived at the Library, the trustees raised the possibility of selling certain prized items, which made him jittery. In a letter to me in January 2015, Gregorian, now the president of the Carnegie Corporation of New York, recalled that, early in his tenure, he went to visit the legendary rare-book dealer Hans P. Kraus in his cluttered shop on East 46th Street:

> I asked for his advice about the Library's rare books and manuscript collection. His advice was to sell them . . . The answer shocked me. Of course, I did not and could not follow his advice . . . I believed that if we started deaccessioning the collection, there would be no incentive for others to donate their collections because they could not be certain that we would keep them. Elected officials could also make the argument that our collections were available to sell whenever there was a need to raise funds.

After the Reynolds, Constable, Gainsborough, and Turner paintings were sold off in 1956, one masterwork remained in the NYPL's collection: Asher B. Durand's 1849 painting, *Kindred Spirits*. It featured Thomas Cole, the founder of the Hudson River School, and William Cullen Bryant, the crusading newspaper editor, poet (he was called the "American Wordsworth"), and civic leader whose energy helped to create both Central Park and the Metropolitan Museum of Art. It was donated to the NYPL by his daughter, Julia, who wrote in a letter in 1908: "I would feel gratified if you can make [*Kindred Spirits*] . . . acceptable to the New York Public Library . . . where, I think, in Bryant Park, [it] will be more at home than anywhere else."

The painting, whose title came from a line in Keats, has fueled the imagination of many critics. Writing in the *Los Angeles Times* in 2006, Rebecca Solnit noted:

> The two stand on a projecting rock above a cataract in the Catskills, bathed like all the trees and air around them in golden light. The painting is about friendship freely given, including a sense of friendship, even passion, for the American landscape itself. In the work of Cole, Durand and Bryant, as in the writing of Henry David Thoreau and Walt Whitman, you can see an emerging belief that the love of nature, beauty, truth and freedom are naturally allied, a romantic vision that still lingers as one of the most idealistic versions of what it means to be an American.

Kindred Spirits, Professor Michael J. Lewis wrote in *Commentary* in 2006, "is itself an exultant précis of local history, both financial and cultural: in 1825 the Erie Canal had opened upstate, making New York City the nation's financial capital even as it made Cole the great witness to the destruction of the Hudson River landscape, which in turn produced the cultural energy that led to the building of Central Park."

The 2004 report recommended that *Kindred Spirits* be sold in a way that honored transparency: "The best approach is to make as complete and fair an analysis as possible; to share and discuss the relevant information candidly and in a timely way; to listen to others very carefully; to seek—if at all possible—a solution that is buttressed by considerable consensus."

This call for transparency and consensus was ignored by President Paul LeClerc. In April 2005, an NYPL official told

Carol Vogel of the *Times* that "any New York institution that wishes to purchase a work will be given preferential payment terms." But the terms of the sealed-bid auction favored wealthy individuals over local museums, such as the Metropolitan Museum of Art, which put forth a losing bid in partnership with the National Gallery of Art.

Kindred Spirits was sold at Sotheby's on May 12, 2005, to Walmart heiress Alice Walton, who reportedly paid $35 million for it. Library staff members learned of the sale just hours before news of it appeared in the press. Nevertheless, the NYPL's trustees expressed satisfaction with the results: according to the trustee-meeting minutes of June 8, 2005, "The price received for the Durand exceeded the record for any previous American painting sold at auction."

Commentators, though, were dismayed. "The Library's art disposals were marred by undue haste," Lee Rosenbaum wrote in *The Wall Street Journal*, noting that the NYPL "engineered the Durand hand-off in a mere month." Michael Kimmelman, then the chief art critic of the *Times*, wrote three scorching essays and described the auction as "a hasty and secretive process that virtually ensured that the work, integral to the city's heritage, would not end up in a New York museum." Kimmelman quoted the Met's director, Philippe de Montebello, as saying, "Closed bids are a horror. If you're an institution, you're terrified to put in millions too much because that would seem irresponsible. Had it been an actual auction we would have had a better chance."

But Kimmelman suggested that the Met could, in fact,

have done much more. "In 1995, when the New-York Historical Society auctioned off art, the New York Attorney General stipulated that certain museums could preempt the purchases, buying for a discount below the hammer price. The Met raised a couple of million dollars to save a Medici salver that the [New-York Historical Society] was disposing of. Durand's picture is at least as integral to the city's heritage. Let its loss be a lesson."

LeClerc scrambled to contain the fallout, informing the *Times* that he was "delighted that [*Kindred Spirits*] didn't leave the country and that it will be in an American museum." But despite the criticism from Kimmelman, Rosenbaum, and others, the trustees pushed ahead and sold a number of other paintings in 2005, including two portraits of George Washington by Gilbert Stuart, one of which had been owned by Alexander Hamilton. One of the Stuart portraits was acquired by a private collector; the other was bought by Walton. That portrait, along with *Kindred Spirits*, is now in the collection of the Crystal Bridges Museum in Arkansas, an institution created from Walton's fortune. (The works by Copley and Peale were also sold.)

The NYPL did keep its promise to use the proceeds to expand its research collection. In a letter to me dated July 22, 2013, the NYPL's spokesman, Ken Weine, wrote:

> Sales of Art properties ultimately resulted in proceeds in excess of $53 million, which have been designated . . . to be used solely for the acquisition of

> Research Libraries materials. The fund has made possible the acquisition of the following collections to name just a few: Maya Angelou Archive, Annie Proulx Papers, Arthur Schlesinger Papers, William S. Burroughs Archive and Martha Swope Collection.

Weine's letter suggests that the furor over *Kindred Spirits* might have been avoided. Had LeClerc taken his case to the public—as his own committee had urged—he could have argued that only a massive infusion of cash from the sale of the art collection could ensure the NYPL's future as a world-class research institution; he could have explained why the William S. Burroughs Archive is of greater value to the NYPL than *Kindred Spirits*. But there was no public consultation.

The sale of Durand's masterwork left behind a putrid smell. Kimmelman, among many others, sensed that an illustrious institution had relinquished the moral high ground, and the *Times* critic issued a stark warning to museum directors in general and the NYPL's trustees in particular: "A steady corrosion of faith in the integrity of institutions will be the long-term price for short-term wheeling and dealing."

3

"The Greatest Project Ever"

A highlight of Lucette Lagnado's childhood in the 1960s was the weekly "pilgrimage" with her mother from Bensonhurst, Brooklyn, to 53rd Street in Manhattan. Their destination was not the Museum of Modern Art—the one-dollar admission fee was too expensive—but a bustling branch of the NYPL across the street called the Donnell Library. "No entrance fees there," Lagnado recalled in *The Wall Street Journal* in 2007.

For an immigrant family from Egypt whose first language was French, the Donnell was a labyrinth of bliss. Lagnado, who later became an esteemed journalist and author, would seize a book of children's stories by Colette, or a novel by Jules Verne, while her mother—"as if under a spell"—would peruse works by Proust and other titans of the French canon. In Cairo, Mrs. Lagnado had been a teacher, librarian, and bookworm. In New York, she confronted a more attenuated existence: "She missed the French novels we could no longer afford to buy."

A dizzying range of foreign-language materials distinguished the Donnell from the other NYPL branch facilities: as one might expect, there were books in Russian, Spanish, German, and Yiddish—but also titles in Basque, Zulu, Hawaiian, Catalan, Indonesian, Swahili, Sanskrit, and Gaelic. In 1964, when the *Times* devoted a story to the Donnell's foreign-language holdings, the department consisted of eight staff members, all of whom were polyglots. "The only time we were stumped," the supervisor said, "was when a man came in speaking Modern Greek. Our Modern Greek specialist had just left."

Generations of young people were enamored of the Donnell, which also contained tens of thousands of books for children, the original Winnie-the-Pooh stuffed animals, and numerous works of art and design—including original papercuts by Hans Christian Andersen and illustrations by N. C. Wyeth for *Robin Hood.* A busy auditorium, along with a deep film collection, enhanced the Donnell's appeal.

The Donnell was not generally seen as architecturally distinguished, and yet in 1996 Robert A. M. Stern, the dean of the Yale School of Architecture, included it on a list of thirty-five Modernist buildings in New York that ought to be landmarked. Nor was the Donnell a world-class research facility. It was an idiosyncratic local institution that, with scant fanfare and few resources, proved essential to a cosmopolitan city.

The library owed its existence to the civic aspirations of Ezekiel Donnell, an enlightened New York cotton merchant, who set aside $1 million in his will for "a reading room, ample and commodious, which shall be open every day in the week to the public, without charge . . . in which young people can spend their evenings profitably away from demoralizing influences." Owing to complications with his will after his death in 1896, Donnell's vision took decades to reach fruition: the Donnell Library was not built until 1955, on land donated by John D. Rockefeller. When it opened, *The New Yorker* observed: "The interior is as warm and cheerful as the living room of a big country house."

The years went by; the NYPL's financial difficulties continued; and the Donnell became a real-estate commodity. On November 6, 2007, LeClerc announced that the NYPL had signed a contract to sell the property to a hotel and travel company that would build a luxury tower on the site. At the base of the tower would be a new, modernized Donnell Library. The profit for the NYPL? $59 million.

The public was never told about the NYPL's negotiations with the company, Orient-Express. Said LeClerc to the *Times*, after the deal was inked: "We looked into the opportunity to capitalize on the asset itself, build a gorgeous new state-of-the-art collection and have a whole lot of money left over for other branches." The building, LeClerc said, was a wreck, and too "shabby" for the upscale block that housed MoMA. The Donnell was closed the following year.

Yet even as the Donnell was being emptied of its remarkable collection, a far more sweeping plan was quietly underway. On March 11, 2008, LeClerc announced a $100 million gift from one of his trustees, the Manhattan financier Stephen A. Schwarzman. That money, according to Robin Pogrebin of the *Times*, would be used to "jump start" a wide-ranging expansion plan forged by the trustees. Schwarzman thought it was a fine idea, and told the *Times*: "This was an absolutely first-class, professional, practical strategic plan, and it deserved to be supported."

What was the essence of this "professional, practical" plan? Mainly it was a set of real-estate transactions propelled by financial duress. There were no more valuable paintings left to sell, so the NYPL's leaders decided to put Library property on the market. The City owned the 42nd Street Library and most of the branch libraries—the NYPL only operates those facilities. But the NYPL owned the land beneath the Donnell Library, and two other Midtown properties: the Mid-Manhattan Library on 40th and Fifth Avenue, and the Science, Industry and Business Library on 34th Street. Selling the latter two would generate a significant price in the booming real-estate market.

The *Times* story on Schwarzman's gift offered a cursory

overview of the burgeoning scheme. It noted that the Mid-Manhattan Library would be sold, and that its holdings would be transferred to the marble structure across the street, which would subsequently have a 100,000-square-foot circulating library alongside its core research collection.

Buried in the twentieth paragraph was news about the building's interior: "The new circulating library will be situated in a vast space that currently houses eight levels of stacks below the Main Reading Room . . . The space [will] be gutted."

This disclosure concerning the fate of the stacks generated sparse public discussion. Seven months later, on October 22, 2008, LeClerc announced that Norman Foster would design the new circulating library at 42nd Street. "It's the greatest project ever," Foster exulted to the *Times*. LeClerc said that Foster's renovation would result in "the biggest comprehensive library . . . in human history."

A new project by Foster, who was keen to expand his presence in Manhattan, inspired supportive commentary about the NYPL's new direction. "I don't blame people for being nervous. It takes a certain hubris to mess with the noble Beaux-Arts structure" at 42nd Street, wrote *New York Times* architecture critic Nicolai Ouroussoff, who is known for his warmth toward "starchitects." But the hiring of Foster, he wrote, "should put our minds at ease." Noting Foster's long history "of designing thoughtful additions to touchy historical structures, including the British Museum in London and the Reichstag in Berlin," Ouroussoff affirmed that the project's value "lies in the delicious tension that could be created between new and old."

For Ouroussoff, Foster's design for the British Museum's Great Court was not radical enough—"he seemed to be striving too hard not to disturb the 19th-century structures"—and the *Times* critic urged Foster, in his blueprint for the NYPL, to "resist timidity." Foster's design would not be released for another four years, but Ouroussoff still concluded his essay with a reverie: "The notion of passing through these magisterial chambers and emerging in one of Mr. Foster's technological marvels makes the mind reel. There is no project today that is more important to the civic identity of New York."

The intellectual architect of the NYPL's metamorphosis, Paul LeClerc, was raised in Bayside, Queens, and educated at Columbia University, from which he received a doctorate in French literature in 1969 with a dissertation on Voltaire. Like Gregorian, LeClerc was a long-time product of academia: for many years, he had been a senior administrator at the City University of New York, but he possessed none of Gregorian's dynamism and in-house popularity. LeClerc joined the NYPL after the sudden death of Father Timothy Healy, Gregorian's successor, a man who gave his NYPL salary to the Jesuits and lived in a bare-bones Midtown apartment. An Oxford-trained John Donne scholar, Healy collapsed of a heart attack at Newark Airport in

1993; his time at the NYPL was brief—just three and a half years.

Eighteen months after LeClerc started at the Library, he was the subject of an upbeat profile in the *Times*. LeClerc, wrote William Grimes, "projects intellectual rigor, a love of books and a technocrat's fascination with the mastery of complex organizational systems." LeClerc emphasized his seamless transition from academe to the NYPL: it was like "slipping a hand into a custom-made glove." (His salary and compensation package would reach $813,345 by 2006, according to the *Times*.)

Around 2003, LeClerc began to think seriously about a radical overhaul at the NYPL involving real-estate sales, consolidation, and fund-raising. He hired McKinsey & Company, whose fee was covered by a grant from the Andrew W. Mellon Foundation. Later, in 2007, Booz Allen Hamilton, a gargantuan consulting firm that derives much of its revenue from the U.S. military and intelligence agencies, would replace McKinsey as LeClerc's preferred consultant.

As he set out to remake the NYPL, LeClerc had a devoted partner, a seventy-year-old real-estate developer named Marshall Rose. Educated at City College and New York University Law School, Rose, the son of a furrier, entered the real-estate business in the 1960s and earned enough money that by 1980 he was able to start a foundation in his own name and that of his wife, Jill. After she died, he married the actress Candice Bergen in 2000. (Marshall Rose is unrelated to longtime NYPL trustee Sandra Priest Rose, who paid for the restoration of the Main Reading Room in 1998, after which it was renamed the Rose Reading Room.)

Enterprising and socially ambitious, Rose, in the 1970s, occupied himself with charitable activities, to which he devoted much of his energy. It was Vartan Gregorian who appointed him to the NYPL's board of trustees: early in his tenure, Gregorian and Heiskell, the board chairman at the time, realized that the Library needed a dependable trustee to oversee its real-estate holdings, which included properties donated by wealthy friends of the institution.

In this fashion, the NYPL's real-estate portfolio was entrusted to Rose. In his memoir, Gregorian called him "a man of high energy and integrity . . . who was ready to share with us his time, his wisdom, and his wealth." Heiskell, in his own book, recalled an unusual gift bequeathed to the NYPL: a garage at 87th Street and Broadway in Manhattan. The NYPL had an offer of $150,000 for it, but, on a hunch, he asked Rose to examine the property:

> [Rose] reported back: don't sell it, something is happening up there. Sure enough, the garage was at the bottom of a building that was about to be demolished to make way for a high-rise. We eventually sold the garage for $3 million. We turned over all real estate to Marshall, put him in charge of all construction, and later made him head of the executive committee. (Ten years later he became chairman of the Library.)

•

Rose did not confine his philanthropic activities to the NYPL, and his reputation grew in Manhattan society. In 1999, Rose was featured in a "Talk of the Town" piece in *The New Yorker*, written by the magazine's architecture critic, Paul Goldberger, which appeared under the heading "GOOD NEIGHBORS DEPT."

Goldberger described Rose as "a kind of real-estate adviser in the public interest . . . who appears to have a hand in everything in New York, but he never leaves fingerprints." Readers learned that Rose had assisted the NAACP Legal Defense Fund in the construction of a new headquarters, and had helped the Central Synagogue with the sale of its air rights. Reflecting on his journey, Rose remarked: "Some people make dresses, I make buildings." He added:

> For example, in the late seventies, I helped the New York City Bar Association, on Forty-fourth Street, which was wasting a whole building with library stacks. I showed them how we could put the books underneath the building, and sell the rest of the building for fourteen million dollars. It was like a Rubik's Cube, moving the spaces around.

LeClerc and Rose, in consultation with Booz Allen, made a consequential decision in 2007: to sell three nearby libraries in Midtown Manhattan. Ironically, one of those facilities—the Science, Industry and Business Library (SIBL) on

34th Street and Madison Avenue—was an institution that Rose himself had helped to create in the early 1990s. "SIBL was Marshall's baby," a former high-ranking NYPL executive told me in 2014.

To pay for this new science and business library, which occupied a landmarked space that once housed the B. Altman department store, Rose contrived a financial arrangement that the *Times*, in 1991, described as "unusual": he convinced thirty corporations and wealthy individuals to guarantee $30 million worth of bonds; the companies included Citicorp, Morgan Stanley, Pfizer, and Revlon; among the wealthy donors was Lewis B. Cullman, who, with his late wife, Dorothy, would become one of the NYPL's leading benefactors, endowing a center for scholars and writers at 42nd Street.

When SIBL opened in 1996, Paul Goldberger, then the *Times*' architecture critic, was there with his notebook. In a front-page review, he wrote that the new Library "is every bit as grand, in its way, as the . . . great main building at Fifth Avenue and 42nd Street":

> There is a sense everywhere of bright openness: in the entry lobby, with a high, undulating wall filled with quotations about business; in the glass and metal elevator enclosure; in the terrazzo and stainless steel stair that takes visitors to the main hall and reading room that are one level below the street but that feel as filled with light and air as a penthouse.

A few weeks later the *Times* published an editorial about SIBL. "The miracle on Madison Avenue," it concluded, "marks a new era for both New York City and its singular library system." The editorial hailed Rose as "a fierce advocate of the Library."

Bad luck plagued SIBL, however: four months after it opened, a fire erupted in an abandoned fur vault deep inside the old department store, and two dozen firefighters collapsed from heat exhaustion. (SIBL's materials were unscathed.)

With 250 computers and 500 work stations, SIBL was designed to be the library of the future: it was intended to be a place to check the price history of a stock, to read a corporation's annual report, or to locate the name and address of a president of a company to whom one could direct a letter of complaint. It was also meant to be a facility devoted to science. But the NYPL's commitment to science was tenuous: by 2011, the institution was no longer collecting scientific materials. It couldn't afford to: annual subscriptions to certain scientific journals are as high as $15,000. Still, SIBL had hundreds of thousands of visitors every year, and many entrepreneurs and researchers remained loyal to it.

Yet just a decade after it opened—at a cost of $100 million, at least one-third of which was borne by taxpayers—SIBL became a liability to those who had built it. The miracle on Madison Avenue was fleeting. Rose's baby would be sold.

•

The other nearby facility that LeClerc and Rose decided to sell was the hulking structure on 40th Street and Fifth Avenue, the Mid-Manhattan Library. Built in 1970, after a long gestation period, it was born from a demographic need: from the 1940s to the '60s, the Main Reading Room at 42nd Street was overrun by students, who sought an atmospheric place to work and materials not available in their high school and college libraries. But there was never enough space in the vast reading room for them.

The Mid-Manhattan was designed to serve the student population with holdings that included 350,000 books on open shelves; 36,000 bound volumes of periodicals; and 10,000 reels of microfilmed magazines, some of which went back to the seventeenth century.

It was renovated in 1982, but the rot set in quickly. By the 1990s, the Mid-Manhattan Library was decaying: the air-conditioning and heating systems were faulty; the carpets were frayed; the bathrooms were malodorous and filthy; and buttons were missing from the elevator panels. For staff members, it was a demoralizing environment; employees even whispered about bedbugs on the premises.

But it was a beautifully proportioned space for a public library at the crossroads of a great city, and New Yorkers flocked to it not only for books, magazines, DVDs, and computer and career services, but also for conversation and repose. Few adored the facility, but 1.5 million people a year used it. That fact mattered little to LeClerc and Rose: the Mid-Manhattan, like Donnell and SIBL, would fare poorly in the new "strategic plan."

•

In 2006, as they conceived the Central Library Plan, LeClerc and Rose faced the challenge of how to pay for it. A "starchitect" for the 42nd Street Library would demand millions—a steep expenditure for an antiquated, poorly financed public library system. A significant infusion of money from the City would be necessary, along with a philanthropic angel who believed in the shining new vision for the NYPL's future and whose commitment to it would inspire other rich donors to send checks.

The benefactor the Library got was not an angel, but a character out of the pages of Balzac or Dreiser—Stephen A. Schwarzman. Schwarzman was born in 1947 in Philadelphia, where his father and grandfather owned a dry goods store, as described by James B. Stewart in a 2008 *New Yorker* profile. When he was a teenager, he beseeched his father to open a second store and become a more ambitious businessman; his father replied that he was satisfied with what he had. Years later, the store failed; the competition from chain stores had become too intense.

Schwarzman floated through Yale, indulging a passion for classical music; he sometimes listened to records for ten hours a day. In his early twenties, he discovered an aptitude for business, and made his way to Lehman Brothers, where he flourished. In 1984, he helped to engineer the sale of Lehman to American Express. A year later, Schwarzman and Peter G. Peterson founded Blackstone, which soon had retainer agreements with Union Carbide, Sony, and Firestone. The alliance between the two men, Stewart wrote, would turn into "one of the most successful and enduring in Wall Street history."

Blackstone was a colossus, with a three-pronged strategy for money-making: private-equity, commercial real estate, and hedge funds. When the company went public in 2007, Schwarzman received $677 million and retained shares worth $7.8 billion.

He is a visible and outspoken billionaire. In 2010, when the Obama administration took steps to tax hedge-fund managers at a higher rate, Schwarzman declared: "It's like when Hitler invaded Poland in 1939." He is fond of lavish parties: the theme of his 2006 Christmas gala was James Bond; models dressed as "Bond girls" worked the room. Schwarzman's sixtieth birthday party, in February 2007, reportedly cost $3 million and featured a full-length portrait of himself. His personal chef told *The Wall Street Journal* that the mogul dines on $400 crab and complains when he hears his employees' shoes squeak.

But the rise in his fortune was not accompanied by an increase in his charitable expenditures, a fact that drew criticism. Stewart reported in *The New Yorker*: "He says that he is pondering a major gift, one likely to silence his critics, but . . . it would be premature to say more." The financier was already on the NYPL board, and a few weeks after Stewart's piece appeared, LeClerc announced the Schwarzman gift. In exchange, he agreed to rename the 42nd Street Library the "Stephen A. Schwarzman Building."

Few strolling past the Library could fail to notice its

new incarnation: when the gift was first reported, LeClerc assured the *Times* that Schwarzman's name would appear in just two places on the façade. But the financier's name was carved into the building's exterior in five prominent locations, a decision that irked historic preservationists. In a written statement in early 2008, the Historic Districts Council, a nonprofit organization, noted that the names of the NYPL's founders (Astor, Lenox, Tilden) appear just once on the building's façade.

The news that the Library would be named after Schwarzman left a dismaying impression on me, yet until 2011 I knew nothing of the NYPL's overhaul: I had overlooked the three *Times* stories describing it. But when the prominent academic librarian mentioned, during my first week of reporting in June 2011, the imminent removal of three million books from the old stacks at 42nd Street, I was keen to know more.

A few days later, on June 29, 2011, I went to see Ann Thornton, the NYPL's top librarian, in her spacious, wood-paneled office at 42nd Street and Fifth Avenue. Nearly three years had passed since journalists—Pogrebin and Ouroussoff of the *Times*—had inquired about the Library's "strategic plan," and Thornton seemed anxious during the interview. A member of the NYPL's public-relations team sat with us, taking notes and occasionally interjecting data about staff layoffs, which she seemed keen to emphasize.

Thornton confirmed what I had heard: millions of books

from the stacks would be sent to a modern offsite storage facility in Princeton; the stacks would be "removed." When I asked her why this was necessary, she replied that the NYPL's aim was to "democratize" the 42nd Street Library and revitalize spaces long closed to the citizenry. She said that in a building of 600,000 square feet, only 32 percent of the space was currently open to public use, and she implied that too much of that available space was being used by one category of users: those doing serious research.

This was a strange argument. The building was already utterly democratic and filled with a remarkable variety of individuals. Why not, I asked, simply reopen the building's many empty rooms and avoid the cost of demolishing the iron-and-steel stacks and replacing them with an expensive new library? She ignored the question.

Months later, when the plan met public resistance, that argument became the raison d'être for the Foster renovation: the building was underutilized and had to be made *accessible* to the broad public, including immigrants and young people. When this reasoning became hard to sustain, NYPL officials came up with two other reasons to justify the urgency of the renovation: first, the stacks had an antiquated climate-control system, and the books, for their own protection, needed to go to a modern facility in Princeton; second, the CLP would improve the NYPL's finances by generating "up to $15 million a year," money that would be used to hire additional librarians, archivists, and curators, whose ranks had been thinned by austerity measures.

Suddenly LeClerc, just back from a meeting at City Hall, burst into Thornton's office, radiating joy. "Here's the news," he declared. "We got the one hundred million dollars from the City. Isn't it just fantastic?" Thornton jumped up and embraced him. "Paul, that's *wonderful*!" When she introduced me as a reporter, LeClerc inquired, with a sly grin: "Are you a *friendly* reporter?" Then he explained the purpose of the $100 million from Bloomberg's administration: "It's for Norman Foster's renovation of this building." With those words, he walked out of the room to share the news with others. LeClerc retired a few days later, seemingly having achieved his legacy. Soon he would have a new job in France, as the director of Columbia University's campus in Paris.

LeClerc had occasion to be high-spirited at the close of his sixteen-year term: Schwarzman's $100 million gift had just been complemented by another $100 million in City capital funds allocated by the City. The financial scaffolding for the impending overhaul—which the trustees privately called "the strategy" and the public would soon know as the "the Central Library Plan"—appeared to be securely in place. But difficulties lay ahead. It was LeClerc's undertaking, but his successor, Anthony Marx, would have to execute it.

4

Hubris and Corporate Logic

In the early 1980s, when Tony Marx was an idealistic student at Wesleyan University, the turbulence sweeping South Africa fired his imagination. Years later he wrote: "Our antiapartheid activism at the time was no doubt naïve in some respects, but it expressed our moral outrage." He wasn't alone in feeling righteous anger: in those years, the campaign against apartheid was the cause célèbre on elite campuses. When Marx graduated in 1984, he flew to South Africa, keen to see, in his words, the place he had been "yelling and screaming about"; he was also, by his own admission, chasing adventure.

He soon chose an academic career in political science, and the subject of his dissertation research, at Princeton, was the internal configuration and ideology of the African National Congress. For five years he traveled back and forth between South Africa and the United States. Those were heady, action-filled days: his residence in 1984, he told me in 2011, was "a commune of blacks and whites living illegally together, where we would get raided, and amazing people would come through hiding from the police."

He was a politically engaged young scholar. In his 1992 book *Lessons of Struggle: South African Internal Opposition, 1960–1990*, Marx paid tribute to "Kgotso Chikane, an eighteen-year-old I helped to hide from the police while he tried to continue organizing his fellow students in Soweto during 1988." Chikane, according to Marx, was later killed by security forces.

In 1990, Marx was hired by Columbia University, which eventually tenured him. But he grew restless. Sitting in libraries, attending academic conferences, drafting articles for scholarly journals—none of this suited him anymore. Says his friend Robert Townsend: "He told me he'd reached the end of a scholarship track, and that he wanted to switch to something else. That's good self-knowledge."

In 2002, Marx's name was given to a search committee at Amherst College, whose trustees were searching for a new president. Only forty-three when he was hired, he arrived at Amherst with a purposeful agenda: to bring greater numbers of non-elite and foreign students into the ranks of one of the nation's most selective colleges.

His goals were achieved: by 2010, non-white and foreign students constituted 43 percent of Amherst's freshman class. Says Richard Kahlenberg of the Century Foundation:

"Marx helped to change the conversation in higher education about diversity, expanding it beyond race to include socioeconomic status. He used his position of leadership and his charisma to bring attention to the idea that having rich kids of all colors wasn't enough."

Marx also turned out to be an adroit fund-raiser. In his eight years at Amherst, the college raised nearly $500 million. Marx himself secured two remarkable gifts—one for $100 million and the other for $25 million.

But serenity eluded him in small-town Massachusetts. Marx's family stayed in Manhattan—his wife, Karen Barkey, teaches sociology at Columbia, and they have two children—and the metropolis beckoned. Hired by the NYPL in late 2010, Marx started the job in July 2011. (His first-year salary and compensation package totaled $781,000.) He appeared to be qualified to lead the Library: his close friends assured me in 2011 that his interests and passions—egalitarianism, public access to information—corresponded to the Library's historic mission. But they also admitted that he had never administered an institution of the NYPL's size and complexity.

A few weeks after my June 2011 conversation with Ann Thornton, in which I briefly met LeClerc, I went to see Marx in the president's office at 42nd Street, a space outfitted with an antique wooden desk, a golden oak conference table, and paintings from the NYPL's remaining art collection.

Marx, casually dressed, greeted me with a beaming smile and a politician's handshake. He seemed eager to manifest sturdy left-liberal credentials: he began the interview with a reminiscence about the most intoxicating course he took in graduate school, a seminar on Antonio Gramsci, the Italian Marxist, taught by the redoubtable left-wing English historian and critic Perry Anderson. "It was *unbelievable*," Marx recalled with animation.

When I asked him about the Library's transformation plan, Marx became somber, and took a moment to ponder his response. "The way I understand it is this," he said of the plan bequeathed to him. "The driver of the idea of a central library plan is that in the back quarter of this iconic building are stacks of books that are rarely used. We can store and get access to those books without having to take the prime space in a prime location in New York City. To the degree that we can make that space available, and replace books with people, that's the future of where libraries are going."

In that first interview, Marx mentioned that as part of his orientation at the NYPL, he intended to visit each of the eighty-eight branch libraries in Manhattan, Staten Island, and the Bronx. I asked to accompany him on one of those excursions, and he consented. On a steamy afternoon in late August, we visited four neighborhood libraries in upper Manhattan, in a vehicle driven by an NYPL manager. Our first stop was the clean, well-lit branch in Inwood, which is near the apartment building where Marx was raised.

Our next destination was the branch on 162nd Street, located in a densely populated, mainly Latino section of Washington Heights. The building looked grim from the outside: the façade's elegant nameplate had been defaced with green and black paint, and the NYPL flag was in tatters; this wasn't exactly what Andrew Carnegie had in mind when he created the NYPL's branch libraries in 1901. But the facility was full of local residents. After giving us a tour, the branch director said to the NYPL's president: "Would you like to see the custodian's apartment?"

Marx hesitated. The expression on his face suggested that inviting a reporter into that space might not be a great idea, but his finer instincts prevailed. As we mounted the stairs to the top of the building, the director explained that when the branch libraries were constructed in the early 1900s, the top floor was given to a custodian, who resided there with his family. The apartment we were about to see had been empty for more than half a century.

The director opened the door, and suddenly we were in the turn-of-the-century Manhattan of Jacob Riis. It was completely dark, except for a few rays of sunlight streaming through dingy windows. I saw rubble, cobwebs, copious amounts of dust, peeling paint, and an ancient tenement bathtub; there were six bedrooms and a capacious kitchen. Why had this space never been renovated and made part of the bustling neighborhood library downstairs? The director replied that there was never enough money to do so.

Later that afternoon we stopped at the once-elegant

George Bruce branch library on 125th Street in Harlem. That building, too, had a custodian's apartment full of cobwebs and dust. I asked the branch director what she would do with the empty apartment if funds were available to renovate it. "I'd use it for a teen center," she said without hesitation. (According to the Center for an Urban Future, a think tank, eleven NYPL branch libraries in Manhattan contain empty custodial apartments on their upper floors.) When I asked her about what her branch needed, she quickly replied: "Ten more computers." In the back corner of the reading room, I noticed that an old yellow bucket was collecting water from a leaky ceiling.

A few weeks later, I went to visit Khalil Muhammad, the young director of the Schomburg Center in Harlem. It was another hot afternoon, and I asked him about the pedestal fan in front of his desk. "It's there because the air-conditioning in this building doesn't work," he replied stiffly.

Library officials told me Foster's renovation would cost around $300 million. In my initial interview with Marx, I questioned him about the need to spend so much money on a single Midtown facility—one that had already received, since 1995, $65 million in repairs to the façade and the Rose Reading Room. If NYPL officials were so keen to spend $300 million, why not use that money to repair the eighty-eight branch libraries—whose facilities needed at least $500 million in structural renovations—or keep all the branch libraries open on Sundays?

I could see the annoyance in Marx's eyes as he replied: "I

won't sacrifice what those branches can do for the opulence of 42nd Street."

The disparities within the system are well known to staff members. A few days after my tour with Marx, I called a former high-ranking NYPL executive, who remarked to me, with anger and weariness: "The trustees don't care about the branch libraries. They only care about the 42nd Street building."

Marx, who declined to be interviewed for this book, may not have realized the extent to which he had inherited a plan with a tangled, tumultuous history—one that NYPL officials have never publicly discussed, but whose contours can be partially discerned from a thousand pages of trustee-meeting minutes that go back to 2005. These documents, which I obtained from the NYPL in 2013 and 2014 under the Open Meetings Law, are not transcripts of the trustee meetings, but detailed summaries of the proceedings. The minutes are full of holes, silences, and ambiguities, but they are also packed with description and data. This trove of documents, written in language that is brisk and bureaucratic, is the best record we have of the NYPL's internal governance.

The minutes do not refer to the "democratization" of the 42nd Street Library, or to book preservation, or to $15 million per year in additional revenue. What the documents do reveal, with the utmost clarity, is that the Central Library Plan, conceived in the boom years preceding the recession of 2008, was a mystifying combination of austerity and devil-may-care overreach; that it bore the fingerprints of two influential, private-sector consulting firms: McKinsey & Company and Booz Allen Hamilton (whose recommendations have never been made public by the NYPL); and that it was pushed along, in absolute secrecy, not by professional librarians but by a tight core group of wealthy trustees from the worlds of finance and real estate.

Those core trustees—led by the developer Marshall Rose—did what came naturally to them: they sold the NYPL's land and took steps to shrink an institution they may have viewed as bureaucratic and inefficient. (About one-third of the NYPL's employees, mostly lower-level staff, are unionized.) Personal enrichment was certainly not the trustees' intention; they were sincere in their desire to assist the Library. It was hubris that drove them forward, and which ultimately led them astray: they believed that corporate logic could be effortlessly applied to a sprawling, decrepit library system.

In June 2007, trustee Roger Hertog—a sharp-elbowed investment banker and one of the nation's most indefatigable conservative philanthropists—circulated a five-page "rationale" that summarized the CLP; it was given to his board colleagues just before the plan was ratified. Hertog's document is short on detail, but it illuminates the corporate mindset of those who were pushing the NYPL into the future:

> Among the Library's most valuable assets is its large portfolio of real-estate holdings, which have been

> developed and maintained over a very long period. We've spent many hours with consultants studying how best to use these assets in order to do as much as possible for our consumers and do it better than ever. We've studied the best practices of the very best companies with geographically diverse points of service, like Net Flix [*sic*], FedEx, and Barnes & Noble. We've learned that we may need to invest more money now to achieve our goals in addition to very large savings in the future.

This document, which is included in the minutes, is the closest thing we have to a justification for the CLP. But the NYPL was not a robust private-sector company like FedEx, and its users weren't necessarily "consumers." Hertog went on to describe "a massive undertaking" that encompassed not only a $300 million renovation of the 42nd Street Library, but also the creation of five ultramodern branch libraries in underserved city neighborhoods, each of which would cost $40 million, and none of which would ever be built. Hertog's vision—which was also LeClerc and Rose's vision—amounted to a $500 million castle in the air, because the NYPL had virtually no money of its own to "invest."

But NYPL officials were determined to try. Taxpayer money would be necessary. In early 2007, LeClerc and the trustees turned to the city's business-friendly mayor, Bloomberg, and requested $350 million in City capital funds. (They also sought $50 million from New York State governor Eliot

Spitzer.) This request for $350 million was a breathtaking display of chutzpah: the trustees quietly hatched a wildly ambitious scheme, set it into motion, and then sat back and waited for the taxpayer money to arrive. Most of it never would.

Under LeClerc's leadership, the NYPL evolved into a more corporate, secretive, and stratified institution. Before he took over, senior librarians were deeply involved in decision-making. After 2003, when McKinsey was hired, those librarians would be supplanted by outside consultants and a tight circle of senior executives with backgrounds in finance. A harbinger of change was the arrival of David Offensend—a supremely confident investment banker—as chief operating officer in 2004. Offensend became a steely proponent and defender of the CLP. And LeClerc would later create a "strategy office" dominated by men with MBAs, whose work seemed opaque to other staffers; the high salaries of its members (in the range of $200,000) generated much water-cooler discussion.

LeClerc and Rose worked closely with three other trustees to implement the Central Library Plan: Roger Hertog; Joshua Steiner, an investment banker who served in Bill Clinton's Treasury Department; and board chairman Catherine Marron, a veteran of Morgan Stanley, Lehman Brothers, and Condé Nast, and the wife of former Paine Webber CEO Donald Marron.

In January 2007, Booz Allen Hamilton was hired to assist the NYPL with its overhaul. A month later, the trustees went into "executive session"—the details of which are always excluded from the printed minutes—to discuss "certain real estate . . . matters." Booz Allen, which was paid $2.7 million by LeClerc, completed its work by May 2007.

The new "strategy" was finalized at two special trustee meetings held in June 2007. At the first, on June 6, LeClerc presented its central "pillar," which entailed "transforming the Library's physical footprint"—bureaucratic language for the sale of NYPL property. COO Offensend stated the matter bluntly: the Library had embarked on a program that entailed the "monetizing of non-core assets."

In the public library milieu, the NYPL has always been seen as careful and deliberate in its decision-making processes. But the trustees, at the behest of their consulting firm, proceeded at full tilt in June 2007: Offensend informed his colleagues at the first special meeting that "Booz Allen, based on its extensive experience with large organizations, recommended that the strategy be implemented *as soon as it is approved by the Trustees*" [italics mine].

Three weeks later, on June 28, 2007, the CLP was ratified; it's not clear if any trustees voted against it. Chairman Marron hailed "the crucial assistance provided to the effort by consultants Booz Allen Hamilton." Marron, who possessed no library expertise, was essential to the whole enterprise: nine months later LeClerc called her "*the* guiding force behind the new plan."

Did Booz Allen conceive of the idea of demolishing the stacks? It seems not. Offensend told me during an interview in July 2013 that the removal of the stacks was first discussed at a meeting (whose date he could not recall) between himself and three top NYPL executives—one of whom was David Ferriero, who was appointed Archivist of the United States by President Obama in 2009 and declined to be interviewed for this book.

The two special trustee meetings in June 2007 occurred under a blanket of secrecy. Marron "reminded all in attendance of the importance of maintaining confidentiality." Why, in a plan involving a library, was "confidentiality" emphasized? A key element of the CLP was the sale of the beloved Donnell Library—a decision, the trustees must have known, that would arouse public indignation. The breadth of the CLP remained concealed for nine months: in her introduction to the Library's 2007 annual report, Chairman Marron referred to it in elliptical terms, and LeClerc's "Letter from the President," in the same document, didn't mention the plan at all.

Meanwhile, the CLP had been quietly rubber-stamped by the City. NYPL officials met with First Deputy Mayor Patricia Harris, one of Bloomberg's most trusted aides, in early 2007; according to the minutes, Harris expressed "initial enthusiasm" about the CLP. (Harris, along with Bloomberg, did not respond to interview requests for this book, and City Hall did not provide documents in response to a Freedom of

Information Law request on the grounds that the material is "exempt from disclosure.")

Months passed before the NYPL's staff was officially informed of the plan: they learned of it in October 2007, four months after it was born. "The NYPL seemed to want to make the whole thing a fait accompli so quickly that no open discussion was tolerated from staff," a retired librarian says. "We were made to feel old and against change. Maybe we were the former, but not the latter!"

Rose moved rapidly to dispose of the Donnell Library. Two bidders emerged: the Kushner family, which owns many properties in Manhattan, and a subsidiary of the Bermuda-based Orient-Express company, which owned the abutting "21" Club. Rose chose the Orient-Express subsidiary, mainly because the parent company—"a corporation with $2 billion in market capitalization"—would "guarantee the transaction."

By early October 2007, the sale of the Donnell was nearly completed, and Rose saw only one potential roadblock: there was a faint chance the building that housed the Donnell could be landmarked, endangering the deal. The minutes of the trustee meeting of October 29, 2007, state: "There are no contingencies to closing other than a landmarking risk which Mr. Rose addressed by informing [the trustees] of his private conversations, and indicating any landmarking risk, in his opinion, was extremely remote." Rose had nothing to fear: city residents didn't know that the Donnell Library was about to be sold.

By late October, Donnell's fate could no longer be concealed: as a public company, Orient-Express was obliged to disclose the agreement within four days of its execution. An announcement was prepared, and its release carefully orchestrated: LeClerc hired one of Manhattan's leading public relations firms, known for its specialty in crisis communications, to contain any fallout. According to the minutes for the trustee gathering of October 29, 2007:

> The public relations offices of the Library and Orient-Express are working together on this matter. Also, a list of anticipated questions from the press and answers has been drafted by the Library . . . Further, the Howard Rubenstein firm has been engaged to advise on this and other public relations matters related to the roll-out of the Central Library Plan.

"An odd mix of culture and commerce" was how Robin Pogrebin described the sale of the Donnell in the *Times* on November 7, 2007, in a story titled "New York Public Library's Donnell Branch to Share Space with Hotel."

Now it was time for LeClerc to find an architect who could transform the 42nd Street building. He contacted Paul Goldberger, who was then the architecture critic of *The New Yorker*, with a request: Would he assist the NYPL in assembling a list of potential candidates? Goldberger said yes. Eight years after his 1999 encomium to Marshall Rose in *The New Yorker*, Goldberger became a paid adviser to the

NYPL's Architect Selection Committee, whose co-chairman was none other than Rose himself. Asked about the payment he received from the NYPL in 2007, Goldberger told me in October 2014: "I cannot comment on the matter of the consulting fee."

The CLP was mainly about real-estate sales, but it was also about fund-raising: the trustees were extraordinarily determined to raise the institution's endowment to $1 billion, and they saw the CLP as a vehicle through which to do that. Nonprofit organizations crave large endowments, which generate revenue for daily operations, and the NYPL's trustees knew their endowment was modest compared to those of other local institutions; the Metropolitan Museum, for example, had a $3 billion endowment in 2007.

Schwarzman's gift—the "lead gift" in the new, $1 billion fund-raising campaign tied to the CLP—was announced at a press conference in the elegant vestibule of the 42nd Street building on March 11, 2008. The first speaker was Toni Morrison, who declined to be interviewed for this book, and whose initial public endorsement of the CLP may have been based on limited knowledge of it. Mayor Bloomberg, in his remarks, saluted "the two greatest benefactors" in the NYPL's history: "At the turn of the century it was Andrew Carnegie. Today it is my friend Stephen Schwarzman."

The next day, when the trustees sat down together in their elegant wood-paneled meeting room, the mood was jubilant: the NYPL, said Chairman Marron, had embarked on a "transformative new strategy . . . a bold, decisive and visionary plan for the Library that will enable it to maintain its greatness and relevance in a changing world." She lauded the "brilliant leadership" of Roger Hertog and Joshua Steiner; Marshall Rose was commended for his "outstanding efforts" on the real-estate front; LeClerc was thanked for his "dedicated work."

At the beginning, the "bold" and "decisive" plan was trouble-free. With the Donnell presumably secure in the hands of Orient-Express, Rose focused his attention on the sale of the tumbledown library at 40th Street and Fifth Avenue, the Mid-Manhattan, for which there was considerable interest from buyers, given the hot real-estate market. He informed the board in May 2008 that the Library had entered into "confidentiality agreements with 35 parties interested in receiving the offering memorandum" for Mid-Manhattan.

But the timing was poor; the market was in turmoil. The minutes for the meeting of June 4, 2008, refer ominously to "the downturn in the economy," which, for the trustees, meant "uncertainty" about the $350 million the NYPL had requested from Bloomberg. Moreover, the controversy that engulfed Governor Spitzer—who resigned after news broke that he had paid for the services of prostitutes—cast doubt on the $50 million from the state. (Those funds never materialized.)

Lehman Brothers crumbled on September 15, and the aftershocks soon reached 42nd Street: Orient-Express was wounded and the Donnell deal had stalled. The minutes for October 6, 2008, note: "Mr. Rose reported . . . that Orient-Express . . . likely will not be able to close . . . given the recent disruption in the credit markets." The Rubik's Cube was stuck. But Rose, with his half-century of Manhattan real-estate experience, wasn't too concerned: "Mr. Rose stated . . . that this was simply a question of timing and that he expected the closing to go forward."

Orient-Express, it turned out, couldn't secure financing. LeClerc hired a law firm to represent the Library in possible legal proceedings, and Howard Rubenstein's crisis-management services were again requested. But Rose was ferociously determined to save the deal, and negotiations between the NYPL and Orient-Express dragged on for two more years, while the property in question, on 53rd Street, remained empty, to the outrage and dismay of citizens who relied on the now-shuttered library. (Donnell's users had been promised a new library, at the base of the luxury tower, by 2012.) Orient-Express finally gave up in early 2011, and took steps to find a buyer to whom it could transfer the contract.

With the economy sinking, Rose raced to unload the Mid-Manhattan Library, for which an undisclosed buyer had been found. On October 6, 2008, the trustees were told that the Democratic candidate for president had a personal connection to the Library. "Barack Obama," Chairman Marron reported, "credited the Mid-Manhattan Library . . . in his efforts many years ago to find work as a community organizer." A few minutes later the trustees voted to sell it. But the deal was doomed: the buyer fled as the financial crisis intensified. The Mid-Manhattan was safe, for a while.

The 2008 recession put Foster's renovation on hold and forced the trustees to concentrate on daily operations, which were threatened by two troubling developments: the City hit the NYPL with a $23 million cut to its operating budget for fiscal year 2010, and the endowment, to the alarm of the trustees, had plunged from $700 million to $500 million, causing a drop in crucial revenue. These headaches forced LeClerc to draw up an emergency blueprint to reduce the NYPL's full-time staff by a staggering 465 positions, about a quarter of the Library's staff.

Cash-flow tribulations also threatened a trio of consequential capital projects: the completion of a new library services center to process books in Long Island City, Queens, the creation of which was a second-tier element of the CLP; the restoration of the 42nd Street façade; and the outfitting of a temporary replacement library for the Donnell in a cramped space on East 46th Street, which turned out to be a very costly proposition—LeClerc and Rose had inked a rental lease whose terms called for payment of $850,000 for the first year (with possible increases thereafter), but the Library also spent nearly $5 million to outfit that new temporary facility.

All of this evoked the dog days of the 1960s and '70s: to

wrap up these projects, the trustees took $15 million from an endowment already depleted by a decline in the stock market.

For the trustees, the recession was a blunt reminder of the fickleness of the City's funding, and they began to fret that Foster's renovation would be doomed at the outset. The meeting minutes of March 11, 2009, note: "The Library is still awaiting word from the City as to its capital support for this initiative, since the plan will not proceed without City support."

The City's threat to slice $23 million from the NYPL's operating budget in 2009 was, at bottom, a political problem, and LeClerc had to find a way to pressure the mayor and the City Council to restore the money to the final budget. He decided to galvanize the public: the NYPL's communications department fashioned an advocacy campaign—involving letter-writing efforts, social media activism, and press outreach—titled "Keep Your Library Open." It worked: 16,500 letters and 8,000 e-mails would be sent to elected officials demanding that budget cuts to the NYPL be averted. But blood was already flowing in the corridors of the Library: in November 2009, the trustees were told by Library executives that 8 percent of the NYPL's workforce had been eliminated. Yet it could have been even worse.

The gap between the grandiose ambitions of the trustees and the fiscal conditions in New York City was starkly evident at the trustee gathering of February 10, 2010, at which Chairman Marron reported that Mayor Bloomberg "has allocated $50 million in City capital funds" for the CLP; the figure would later grow to $150 million. Certainly this was the outcome LeClerc and Rose had wished for. But the applause must have felt fleeting, because the mayor simultaneously proposed a startling 20 percent cut to the Library's operating budget for the fiscal year ending June 2011. A reduction of that size forced the trustees to contemplate a bleak scenario: the layoff of one-third of the staff, the closing of ten branch libraries, and a drastic curtailment of Library hours. (This would prove, at least in part, to be a false alarm: to LeClerc's relief, most of the City funds were restored at the end of the budget process.)

What mattered most was this: despite the scale of the proposed budget cuts, Mayor Bloomberg had resuscitated the dormant CLP, which prompted LeClerc, in October 2010, to establish an "aggressive timeline" to move it forward; the trustees hoped to have a preliminary design by early 2011. Foster pushed ahead with master planning, and the NYPL hired an eminent structural engineering firm to prepare the stacks for demolition.

But the fiscal woes continued to deepen: the NYPL confronted a $6 million budget gap for 2012, forcing further cuts that LeClerc called "painful." The never-ending fiscal crunch gave rise to soul-searching at the March 2011 trustee gathering: "QUESTION: At what point does the Library lose so many employees that it cannot meet its mission? RESPONSE:

It may be necessary to set a new strategy . . . QUESTION: [Does] the issue of branch closings . . . remain [an] 'untouchable' issue? RESPONSE: There would be great political pain."

The NYPL's finances were a in grim shape, but the trustees kept moving forward with their CLP. It was a Bloomberg-era project and Bloomberg's term was winding down. At the meeting on March 16, 2011, Rose, fully engaged as always, announced that the festering Donnell problem had been straightened out: the contract had been transferred from Orient-Express to a pair of real-estate entities: Starwood Capital Group, based in Greenwich, Connecticut, and Tribeca Associates of Manhattan, who would erect a tower containing both a luxury hotel and high-priced apartments on the site of the old Donnell library. The NYPL would get the $59 million it had sought for the 53rd Street property—an immense relief to LeClerc and Rose.

With that deal in place, Rose argued that it was time to put another "non-core asset" back on the market: "Due to increases in retail property on Fifth Avenue," he told the trustees, "the value of Mid-Manhattan has also probably increased."

By 2011, the NYPL was reeling from budget cutbacks and staff reductions. Instead of Foster's $300 million project, prudent cost-cutting measures, combined with cool-headed management, were urgently needed: bloated executive salaries might have been trimmed (NYPL vice presidents are paid $315,000); foundations might have been approached for support; a public campaign to stabilize City funding could have been initiated. LeClerc might even have consulted New Yorkers about a plan to sell one facility—SIBL on 34th Street—and channel the proceeds back into the NYPL's daily operations.

None of these measures, according to the minutes, were ever considered: the CLP was the only way forward, and the trustees held Foster in a tight embrace; eventually, they would pay him $9 million. In early 2011, bringing matters full circle, LeClerc, to complement the $50 million he already had, requested $101 million in capital funds from the Bloomberg administration—money that was allocated (i.e., promised) to the NYPL on June 29, 2011, the afternoon on which I happened to be visiting the Library's executive suite. LeClerc was ebullient, but also acutely conscious of the fact that he was embarking on a lavish building project at a moment when the old, nagging fiscal problems seemed intractable: in remarks to the trustees four months earlier, he had emphasized "the challenges in public sector funding . . . that seem unlikely to abate anytime soon."

Of the NYPL's sixty trustees, only a handful were intimately involved in the execution of the Central Library Plan. But none of them have shed light on its origins or their own motives. Rose, Hertog, Marron, Steiner, and Schwarzman all declined to be interviewed for this book. Steiner phoned me in August 2013 to say: "For better or worse, I don't talk to journalists." (Marron, Rose, and Steiner would not even provide me with copies of their résumés.)

On several occasions, Neil Rudenstine, the former Harvard University president who succeeded Marron as chairman in 2012, offered to share information with me off the record—on the condition that I not use it—but refused to speak on the record; I declined his offer. Despite many requests since 2011, LeClerc has never made himself available to me for an interview.

5

"An Invitation to Act"

My story, "Upheaval at the New York Public Library," appeared in *The Nation* in early December 2011, more than four years after the CLP was quietly ratified by the trustees. It highlighted the decaying branch libraries; the potential damage to the architectural integrity of the 42nd Street landmark under the CLP; and the weakening of the NYPL's research capacity as a result of the transfer of three million books to the storage facility in Princeton.

"The whole building is a single architectural masterpiece," a Library staff member told me over lunch in an Irish pub in Midtown in July 2011. "The CLP would basically destroy half the library." When I contacted Charles Warren, a Manhattan architect who cowrote a 2006 book about Carrère and Hastings, he observed:

> The building is a machine for reading books in. The stacks are part of what the building is. There's an idea there: that the books are in the center and they rise up out of that machine into the reading room to serve the people. It's a whole conception that will be turned on its head by ripping out the stacks. It's a terrible thing to do.

Staff members insisted that removing three million books would be injurious to scholarly research, because it would slow the pace of moving from one book to another, make spontaneous visits more or less pointless, and add a significant burden of advance planning for out-of-town scholars and users. Indeed, scholars seemed surprised to discover that so many books were leaving 42nd Street for Princeton. When I mentioned the number to David Levering Lewis, a New York University historian twice awarded the Pulitzer Prize, he told me, "We would need to review that very carefully, and perhaps resist it."

It turned out that the NYPL's metamorphosis didn't just involve real estate, architecture, and fund-raising; the collections, too, were being reorganized in ways that were generating anxiety in scholarly circles. In 2008, LeClerc had dissolved two specialist divisions at 42nd Street—the Asian and Middle Eastern Division, and the Slavic and Baltic Division—in a move that brought with it the loss of two charming, old-fashioned reading rooms. The Slavic Reading Room—in which Leon Trotsky and Vladimir Nabokov had worked, and to which Václav Havel and Mikhail Gorbachev had paid visits of tribute—was, to many, a cherished space. In a 1987 event honoring the Slavic Division, George F. Kennan had referred to the reading room's "cathedral-like ambience."

Historically, the Slavic Division had been a sanctuary for those in flight from tyranny. According to the NYPL's 1942 annual report: "Within the last year or two it has also become something of an intellectual haven for exiles from conquered Poland, Czechoslovakia and Yugoslavia, as well as for the Russian scholars and journalists who had expatriated themselves at the beginning of the Soviet era."

LeClerc's scalpel had reached one of the institution's vital organs: among the Slavic Division's 750,000 holdings is the first book printed in Moscow, the "Anonymous" Gospels; a first edition of Tolstoy's *War and Peace*; and John Reed's personal collection of broadsides and posters from the Russian Revolution.

Library officials said in 2010 that financial duress had forced the closure of the two divisions, which resulted in the loss of several experienced and admired curators. But staff members, in conversations with me, chose to highlight the way in which the divisions were treated: "It was a stealth closure, a fait accompli," one Library employee remarked. "It was done in a way to prevent protests." (The Slavic materials remain in the NYPL's possession, but the staff responsible for them was stripped to the bone.)

The elimination of the two divisions was evidence of a

robust new populism at 42nd Street, a subject about which departing staff members were candid. Early in my research for my story, a librarian urged me to track down Marilyn Johnson's *This Book Is Overdue! How Librarians and Cybrarians Can Save Us All* (2010), in which she interviewed John M. Lundquist, the bruised former curator of the NYPL's Middle Eastern division, who said:

> Our division has been dissolved. Our reading rooms have been closed. Our librarians have been reassigned . . . In theory, we continue as collections, the Asian and the Baltic, but I'm highly skeptical . . . The whole library has been drastically downsized . . . There has been nothing about this in the press, no. Obviously the library doesn't want any publicity . . . They foresee many thousands more people in this building, and that, to them, is a worthy goal. There is a perception that libraries are archaic, dead, outdated, and that everything is now on the Internet, in digital form. We [librarians] are old, stooped-over people, doing old, stooped-over things. [The NYPL administration] want[s] to lighten things up, they want the library to be active and hip.

On the record, NYPL executives were tight-lipped in response to my inquiries. On background, they were willing to say a bit more, always alluding to the money crunch. "We need to get more efficient," one executive told me. "Our sources of revenue from the City and the state are not keeping up with inflation. We've got to find ways to structurally reduce our costs."

Late in the evening of November 7, 2011, after my story was filed but before it was published, a City official told me that Marx had just been arrested. The next day *the New York Post* published a piece headlined "READ HIM HIS RIGHTS: LIBRARY PREZ 'DWI.'" It began:

> Booked!
>
> The president of the New York Public Library was busted for drunken driving after careening in reverse down an East Harlem Street Sunday in a bid to maneuver around the marathon—but ended up slamming his luxury car into a sanitation truck . . . More than an hour later, he allegedly blew a .19 on a blood alcohol test—more than twice the legal limit of .08.

According to a witness interviewed by the *Post*:

> "He just kinda came out of nowhere!" said sanitation worker Franklin Hernandez, who was sitting in his truck on 138th Street, between Madison and Fifth avenues, when Marx made his bizarre move.
>
> "He was going pretty fast. He just missed the truck

in front of me and then, bam! He smashed into my truck.

"I jumped out, and he tried to put the car in drive—I just stood there in front of him, put my hand up and said, Do not move that car!"

On December 9, 2011, Marx, who was driving an Audi registered to the NYPL, pleaded guilty in Manhattan Criminal Court. Judge Jennifer Schecter ordered him to attend sixteen counseling sessions and to pay a $500 fine; his license was revoked for six months.

Before confronting the judge, Marx had to face the Library's sixty trustees, who went into executive session to discuss the accident; the minutes do not record what was said. Marx was taken to the gallows, but he didn't hang: he remained the president and CEO of the NYPL. He has never discussed the details of the car accident, except to say: "I deeply regret embarrassment caused to my family and to the New York Public Library." Two days after his arrest, I called one of his closest friends, who sounded shaken by Marx's travails. "This is serious," he remarked. "Tony could have killed someone." A few weeks earlier, this friend had told me what was uppermost in Marx's mind in his first months at the NYPL. "What to do with the building," he said, "and how to manage sixty trustees."

Indeed, the accident didn't make his dealings with those trustees any easier. Some large nonprofit organizations are staff-driven, and trustees play a secondary role. The NYPL, by contrast, is board-driven, and the trustees wield enormous power. Staff members believe Marx's arrest weakened his power vis-à-vis the trustees, and lessened his inclination to challenge a plan he had inherited from them. The accident diminished him externally, too: the man whose job was to sell a $300 million renovation project to a skeptical public was now in possession of a criminal record.

Hours after my story appeared in December 2011, LeClerc—retired from the NYPL, but prominently featured in my narrative—made an outraged phone call to *The Nation*'s editor and publisher, demanding corrections to the piece. Vanden Heuvel advised him to write a letter to the editor, which LeClerc never did. There was no official response to the story from either Marx or the Library's communications department.

My story didn't halt the forward march of the CLP, but it inspired enough attention for the trustees to open a window. At their meeting of February 15, 2012, they decided to initiate a "public engagement process"; then they authorized Foster to proceed with schematic design, a fact that was reported the next day by Robin Pogrebin in a *Times* story titled "Ambitions Rekindled at Public Library." "The whole project has got enormous vitality," Schwarzman told Pogrebin. "When it's completed, people are going to be dazzled."

Pogrebin's article generated eighty-four online comments, most of which were caustic. "This is simply nonsensical and atrocious," wrote one reader. "What an abomination," chimed in another. "The plan has all the earmarks of calamity," wrote a third. Other readers were encouraged. "Books are becoming less and less what a library is about," one person wrote. "I applaud the move."

A few weeks later, I was invited to appear on a flagship public-radio program in New York City, WNYC's *Leonard Lopate Show*, which is devoted to politics, culture, history, and science. It's a uniquely cerebral space in the public-radio milieu, and Lopate brings an edgy brilliance to his two-hour daily program.

Next to me in the studio was Caleb Crain, a forty-seven-year-old critic and scholar who writes for *The New Yorker* and other publications and who, in 2002–03, had been a fellow at the NYPL's prestigious Dorothy and Lewis B. Cullman Center for Scholars and Writers, where, for a year, individuals are given the means to pursue a book-length project. Crain knew the 42nd Street building well: for a long time he had used its collections and observed its internal rhythms and dynamics, some of which left him dismayed. When *Kindred Spirits* was sold, Crain wrote on his blog, *Steamboats Are Ruining Everything*: "Before the painting vanished, I hadn't known how much I would miss it. I wonder if the trustees have applied too rigorously the business principle of pruning down to the core."

The WNYC interview lasted thirty minutes, and Crain, who has a doctorate in English from Columbia University, expressed cautious misgivings about the burgeoning CLP. "The Library is changing direction," he said. "If you make it more difficult for researchers to do work there, there will be a certain slippage of quality." He noted that, under a new pilot program, vetted researchers could, for the first time, leave the building with books from 42nd Street's vast research collection—a change of policy that left some staff members incredulous; they worried, rightly, that books could be damaged or lost. When he signed up for the pilot program, a Library employee took his paperwork, shook his head, and remarked with a sigh: "You, too, have gone over to the dark side, Caleb?"

Three days after our radio appearance, Crain wrote a lengthy blog post titled "Build More Deliberately," in which his caution receded and thorny questions floated to the surface:

> To put my concerns bluntly: What problem is the Central Library Plan meant to solve? It will cost $350 million, it will disrupt the research library during construction, and it will permanently impair the ability of the research library to serve scholars . . . Is it to make the 42nd Street building more democratic? . . . Is the goal of the CLP to make available more internet access? . . . Is the goal to bring literacy education to children? . . . Is the goal to save money?

If the intention was to anchor the NYPL in the digital age, then, Crain pointed out, it was time to revisit the inglorious history of the SIBL:

> [SIBL] was installed in 1996 in the hope that local proprietors of small businesses would be attracted by

> access to CD-ROMs and online databases. This was a bold guess about the future of information technology, and like most bold guesses about the future, it turned out to be a little off target . . . The lesson, perhaps, is that cultural institutions like the New York Public Library shouldn't aspire to be bleeding-edge.

In the months to come, Crain's blog posts and tweets would be animated by a deep concern for the fate of the NYPL's research mission, and for the need to preserve access to books and materials on paper. He quickly ascertained that the CLP favored e-books over paper books, most of which were headed to Princeton, New Jersey:

> What if it turns out that the e-book is a great invention for reading as a consumer, but not much use for reading as a scholar? What if it turns out that it's simply not possible to apprehend a book in electronic form the way it can be apprehended in print form? I know that whenever I try to imagine reproducing my scholarly methods electronically, I halt at the problem of how to reproduce digitally the phenomenon of having a dozen physical books open to different pages at once on my work table. In the future, will I need to buy a dozen iPads? Why not wait to reconceive the library until we know a little more about how scholars will use books and e-books in the digital age?

On WNYC, Crain had referred to the "slippage" of the NYPL's research capacity, a subject to which he returned, with sparkling detail, in "Build More Deliberately":

> I've translated Czech literature and written about it . . . During my fellowship year, I gave the [Slavic] division a set of Czech literary journals that I thought they would be better custodians of than I could be . . . In preparation for the Leonard Lopate show, I tried a simple test: I looked up the recent winners of three Czech literary prizes: the Jiri Orten Prize, the Jaroslav Seifert Prize, and the Magnesia Litera Prize for book of the year. It turns out that the New York Public Library has no copies of the books that won these prizes in the past three years. And as it happens, the book that won the Jaroslav Seifert Prize *four* years ago was the eighth and final volume of Václav Havel's collected writings. The NYPL doesn't have that book, either—an embarrassing lacuna not only on account of Havel's importance as a politician and writer but also because Havel gave a signed copy of the first seven volumes to the library in person in 2003.

His conclusion was resolute: if the NYPL could not safeguard its materials, it should relinquish them:

> The library's core collection remains as indispensable to scholars as ever, and the ideal of the library—the

> belief that anyone should be able to walk in off the street and find out as much about a topic as has ever been published—is not susceptible to "metrics." . . . If [NYPL] is abandoning its research mission, the larger community of writers and scholars should be alerted. Should the research collection and its buildings be given to the federal government, and operated as a second campus of the Library of Congress? If the library isn't abandoning that mission, it needs to renew its dedication to it.

Crain's blog post was seen by his wide circle of friends and colleagues in journalism and academia, including Alex Ross, a critic for *The New Yorker*, and Lorin Stein, the editor of *The Paris Review*. (Ross posted a brief item on his website about the row; Stein, in a paragraph on *The Paris Review*'s website, asked why it was necessary to "tear out seven floors of stacks.") Other colleagues responded to the news with poisonous darts aimed at Marx. On March 28, 2012, Scott McLemee, a columnist for *Inside Higher Ed*, published an essay titled "Stop Cultural Vandalism":

> I am by no means hostile to e-reading, which certainly has its place. But that place is wherever you happen to be doing it, at the time. The reading possible at the 42nd Street Library is far more location-specific. It is a distinct kind of public-intellectual space, where a reader coming from anywhere in the world can sit

> down with the very copy of a book that Alfred Kazin or M. N. Roy studied there decades ago . . . The links so created are not hyperlinks. And what makes the CLP worrying—beyond its consequences for one research library, however important—is the massive devaluation of "offline reading" it represents . . . The belief that every pre-existing cultural and intellectual expression must be digitized or else downgraded is destructive.

In a cautious letter written in response to the *IHE* essay, Marx offered several new proposals that he may have thought would be catnip to McLemee's academic audience: designated space at 42nd Street for four hundred scholars and writers, and a later closing time of 11 p.m. (The building was then open until 8 p.m. two nights each week.)

Meanwhile, the news about the NYPL's plan was circulating, and polemics were soon matched to satire. On April 7, 2012, radio bard Garrison Keillor used his fictional detective, Guy Noir, to address the NYPL controversy on *A Prairie Home Companion*. In the segment, Guy Noir has been hired by a Manhattan client keen to sell his "big one bedroom" apartment for $11 million. Rumor has it that an elusive Russian "natural gas multibillionaire" from Siberia might be interested in purchasing the unit. "Go find me that Russian," Noir is told.

Noir races around New York City in search of a Russian accent, and finally shows up at the 42nd Street Library—"to see if anybody had taken out Pushkin recently." A hunch-backed librarian, whose name is Igor, uses an old elevator to bring the gumshoe deep into the "sub-sub-sub basement, in the stacks":

> NOIR: And then I saw the forklift. A guy in a hard hat was running it and it was scooping up stacks of books and putting them on a conveyor belt that carried them off down a dark passageway. It was like a coal mine except they were mining books. IGOR: We are clearing out all the books. But here are the Pushkin over here. NOIR: How can they clear out the books? It's a library. IGOR: Nobody reads old books. Only new books. Only on iPad and Kindle. NOIR: But you've got millions of books down here. IGOR: Three million. Maybe four. NOIR: This is a world-class library. IGOR: World-class warehouse. NOIR: What are they going to do with the space? IGOR: It's valuable real estate. Parking ramp and condos. NOIR: Where are the books going? IGOR: To Turtle Mountain in North Dakota. NOIR: There are no mountains in North Dakota. IGOR: There will be when these books get out there.

The ferocity of the controversy caught the trustees by surprise. In a December 2012 article for *Vanity Fair*, whose staff he joined after leaving *The New Yorker*, Paul Goldberger wrote: "They were startled to discover that they were not being hailed for saving the library. They were being accused of destroying it." The trustees hit the accelerator, nevertheless. The minutes for May 16, 2012, state: "Dr. Marx reported that the 'listening process' will continue during the coming months but noted the importance of also moving forward with discussions with Foster."

In March 2012, Joan Scott, a noted historian at the Institute for Advanced Study in Princeton, read my *Nation* story and was shaken by it. The article, she recalled in 2014, "was an invitation to act" in defense of an institution "that matters to me more than almost anything else." In the 1950s, the NYPL helped to fuel Scott's interest in French history: as an undergraduate, she frequented the 42nd Street building, where staff members allowed her to read newspapers that had appeared in Paris during the Revolution of 1848. Some were in fair condition; others turned to dust in her hands. She still remembers "the sheer excitement of touching real paper from ages gone by."

By the time Scott completed her doctorate in French history and entered the job market in 1969, the feminist movement was surging on campuses, and her passion for France was soon matched by an interest in gender. Her first book, published in 1974, was about the glassworkers of Carmaux, but Scott's rising feminism, and her interest in language, led her, under the influence of the historian and philosopher Michel Foucault, in new scholarly directions. She became a leader in her field, pioneering a women's history that was theoretically informed but also faithful to the left-wing roots of labor history.

Her books and articles have influenced feminist scholarship in disciplines such as literature, anthropology, and sociology, and she lectures at universities around the world. In 1985, she became only the second woman appointed to the permanent faculty at the Institute for Advanced Study, where scholars and scientists devote themselves entirely to research on a verdant campus in Princeton that once housed Albert Einstein and J. Robert Oppenheimer.

Scott told me that in 2012, she found herself "feeling angrier and angrier about—I don't know what to call it—neoliberal capitalism and feeling powerless to affect it." For decades, Scott's activism—building women's studies departments, defending academic freedom—had been confined to academia. But as she learned more about the CLP, she found herself ready—and eager—to venture off campus. "She was looking for something," says her son A. O. Scott, a film critic for *The New York Times*. "The Institute for Advanced Study is a very quiet place."

After reading my *Nation* story, Scott called an old friend, Stanley Katz, who was down the road at Princeton University's Woodrow Wilson School, and whose ears were attuned to her lament about the NYPL. In the realm of higher education, Stanley Nider Katz wears many hats (though he prefers elegant bow ties): elder statesman, power broker, commentator, activist, maverick. A member of Harvard's class of 1955 and an ardent old-school liberal, he has numerous friends in the highest echelons of journalism, philanthropy, and politics, and he maintains a punishing schedule of writing, speaking, and traveling that would challenge a person half his age.

Katz is not only an esteemed legal historian, but also an expert on the nonprofit sector, and he was curious about the NYPL's trajectory in the post-LeClerc period. Indeed, Katz had known the young Tony Marx at Princeton; later he extolled his accomplishments at Amherst College. Like Scott, Katz had an emotional attachment, colored by romanticism, to the library at 42nd Street. As a graduate student and young professor, he had relied on the NYPL's resources—especially the old American History Room at 42nd Street, which was abruptly shuttered in 1980, over the objections of scholars like Arthur Schlesinger Jr., who complained about a "rather mysterious" decision-making process at the NYPL. The loss of that intimate room, with its open shelving and camaraderie, is still keenly felt by Katz. "It was a refuge, a haven, an incredible resource," he says. "I could be sure that every reference work that existed was there and available."

Scott and Katz decided to co-author a protest letter, which read in part: "We are alarmed by the Central Library Plan, which seems to us to be a misplaced use of funds in a time of great scarcity." Scott didn't know how to create an online petition, so the letter was dispatched from her personal e-mail account on April 4, 2012. A few dozen scholars, she hoped, would sign the letter, and indeed, the first people to respond were old friends and former students at Columbia, Brown, and CUNY. But a week later, Mario Vargas Llosa e-mailed her from Peru and asked that his name be added.

Five days later, there was another e-mail: "Please add my name to your good letter. Many thanks, Salman Rushdie." Tom Stoppard signed, as did other major writers, including Donna Tartt, Colm Tóibín, Jonathan Lethem, Peter Carey, Adrian Nicole LeBlanc, Ann Patchett, and Amitav Ghosh. Leading historians, too, signed Scott's letter: Anthony T. Grafton, David Nasaw, Jackson Lears, Natalie Z. Davis, and Ramachandra Guha.

Scott was accustomed to receiving a dozen e-mails a day, but now she was waking up to hundreds of messages. Her protest letter would ultimately generate about two thousand signatures, many of them from scholars at prestigious universities around the world who were alarmed about the transfer of millions of books to offsite storage in Princeton.

Other critics of the NYPL were waiting in the wings. On May 9, 2012, *n+1* magazine published a 14,000-word treatise about the Library, "Lions in Winter," by a young freelancer, Charles Petersen, who had written a shorter piece on the topic for *New York* magazine in early 2010 that was subsequently killed. But Petersen couldn't let go of his subject, and continued to work on his NYPL story for another year and a half, trying all the while to sell it to an A-list magazine.

"There was a long time in there when I felt like something of a madman," Petersen says. "I'd walk around telling people, the New York Public Library is destroying itself, and no one knows!" Finally, in the spring of 2012, *n+1* (where Petersen was an unpaid associate editor) agreed to publish his essay at monumental length. He didn't receive a cent for it.

Petersen was lucky: early in his reporting, he made a favorable impression on Paul LeClerc, after which he "basically had carte blanche to interview anyone I wanted" in 2010 and early 2011. He talked to a wide range of staff members, from high-level executives down to librarians, curators, and archivists. He also talked to outside consultants.

"Lions in Winter" was not only a plangent love letter to the NYPL, but also a revealing X-ray of a library that was, to a considerable extent, discarding its research function and transforming itself into a quasi-populist institution propelled by metrics and overseen by ill-defined, highly paid "strategists." After the crash of 2008, many seasoned curators, archivists, and librarians left the NYPL under a voluntary "separation incentive program"—at the same time, Petersen discovered, that the ranks of executives and "strategists" had ballooned at the Library.

The collision between old-school library values and McKinsey/Booz Allen–style efficiency was a principal theme of Petersen's inquiry. One former staff member told him that the NYPL is "applying methodologies and analytic tools that are . . . best suited to a Starbucks or a Walmart. For your collection of Dickens, so what, you get four readers a year, is that relevant? You're supposed to be a research library."

Petersen's essay drew attention to the amorphous nature of the population that came to the NYPL for in-depth research: in many cases, these were self-motivated individuals without access to the libraries of Harvard, Columbia, the Library of Congress, and other world-class research facilities. A typical user of the NYPL's research libraries, one former NYPL executive told him, is "well educated but poor"—a description that applied to Petersen and innumerable other independent scholars, writers, and autodidacts who have passed through the NYPL's doors.

Petersen's conclusion was stark:

> If the reconstruction goes through, scholarly research will be more, not less, concentrated in the handful of inordinately wealthy and exclusive colleges and universities. The renovation is elitism garbed in populist rhetoric . . . Leave the heavy lifting to the folks at Harvard and McKinsey (and the quants in our commodities division), the financiers are saying; for the rest of you, there will be lovely sun-filled spots to check your e-mail.

On May 22, 2012, *n+1* sponsored a panel discussion about the growing NYPL controversy at the New School, in Greenwich Village. The room was full; people were turned away at the door. Two NYPL trustees were seated in the front row: Chairman Rudenstine and Robert Silvers, the editor of *The New York Review of Books*. In the audience were Michael Kimmelman of the *Times*; Crain and Katz; a contingent of librarians; reporters from NPR, *The Wall Street Journal*, and *The New York Times*; and people like the architect Charles Warren and the activist Zack Winestine, who, months later, would lead a group whose aim was to resist the CLP.

NYPL officials initially declined *n+1*'s invitation, but Joan Scott and Stanley Katz convinced Marx that the NYPL should participate in the New School debate. A day before the event, they had sat down with Marx, who had e-mailed them on April 16, 2012, after another *Times* story came out underlining the petition and the early resistance to the plan from scholars. Marx knew Katz, and was eager, at this early stage in the controversy, to engage with him. "I clearly need more advice," Marx had written, "on how to decide and adjust plans going forward." It was not a productive meeting, but Scott and Katz persuaded him to participate in the event.

Early the next morning, the moderator, Eric Banks, learned that the NYPL would send two representatives: Marx and Robert Darnton. Darnton, a longtime NYPL trustee, is the most distinguished scholar on the NYPL's board: he is an eminent historian of France, an authority on the history of the book, and the University Librarian at Harvard. A week earlier, Darnton had published a ringing defense of the CLP in *The New York Review of Books*, and his presence at the

New School was an unmistakable sign that the NYPL meant business.

Marx, in a dark-blue blazer and a light-blue open shirt, and glasses that perched low on his nose, kicked off the panel discussion by saying, "We have no interest in the destruction of the research side of the New York Public Library. But the status quo can't be maintained." The CLP, he said, was essential for three reasons: the Mid-Manhattan Library was rotting; the books were deteriorating in the old stacks under the Rose Reading Room, owing to an "outdated climate-control system"; and the renovation was essential to the NYPL's fiscal health, since the plan would "generate up to fifteen million dollars a year." Marx knew that scholars were upset about the removal of three million books from the stacks, but he expressed confidence that books could be delivered by truck from Princeton to 42nd Street in twenty-four hours. (Regular users who requested offsite books knew that the journey could take up to five days.)

At the end of his remarks, Marx hinted at a compromise—in the form of additional shelving in the book stacks below Bryant Park, adjacent to the Library, a space that already held 1.5 million books. If a second level of shelving in that underground facility was constructed, the bulk of the NYPL's collection could, he suggested, remain on-site. As for the CLP's schedule, it had to get going very soon—"while this [mayoral] administration and this City Council are in office." Bloomberg's successor, Marx seemed to imply, could redirect the $150 million in City capital funds previously allocated to the NYPL.

Darnton, dressed in an elegant black suit and a striped red tie, began with a personal reminiscence: in 1964, as a young reporter for *The New York Times*, he had slipped away to the Main Reading Room during his lunch hour to examine rare pamphlets from eighteenth-century France. But hard times had descended on the Library that nourished him in the 1960s. "NYPL is under unrelenting financial pressure," said Darnton. "We cannot maintain three buildings in Midtown Manhattan. If we do not consolidate them into one building, the research library will continue to decline." (Darnton added that the NYPL's creation of SIBL in 1996 was "a mistake.") Like Marx, Darnton insisted that the old stacks at 42nd Street could no longer provide sufficient protection for the books, which needed to be moved immediately to a modern storage facility.

A quartet of critics took aim at Marx and Darnton. Joan Scott paid tribute to the NYPL as an uniquely democratic research library—one that stands in contrast to some of the eminent research libraries of Europe, which, she emphasized, are not accessible to ordinary citizens. Charles Petersen challenged Marx's assertion that $15 million per year would be generated, noting that the Library's COO, David Offensend, had told him the real figure was closer to $7 million. Concluded Petersen: "The proposed plan is radical: no other library in the country has done anything like this, it is not farsighted, it's not the best of all possible worlds, it's not a tragic necessity. The library must do better." (The critics had no concrete suggestions as to how the NYPL might acquire the extra $15 million per year that it sought.)

The most impassioned critic on the panel was David Nasaw, author of a celebrated 2006 biography of Andrew Carnegie. "We are being told," Nasaw said, "that the only way to save the library is to rip out its innards and transport millions of books to New Jersey." He dismissed Marx's pledge of twenty-four-hour delivery: "If for the past ten years the library has *not* been able to provide reliable twenty-four-hour service, why are we to believe that with additional books moved there, it will be able to do this? Is the traffic on the New Jersey Turnpike going to decrease?"

Nasaw was unsparing: "I'm enough of a New Yorker to understand how the city works and how decisions are made, and what sort of voices speak loudest when large-scale, multimillion dollar projects like this are formulated behind closed doors." He went on:

> I'm not talking about Tony Marx or Bob Darnton, who were given this plan. But I would not be shocked to learn that among the voices that were heard loudest were the city's real-estate interests, deputy mayors, offices of the New York State Economic Development Corporation; politicians who will be running for office and politicians who want to leave behind legacies; architects who seek out large-scale campuses for their work, engineers who believe they can do the

> impossible, planners and numbers crunchers and traffic consultants and hedge-fund managers and wealthy New Yorkers who want their names on buildings . . . and *some* donors, who, motivated by a 21st-century social Darwinism, believe that having made money or being born with it renders them more fit than the rest of us to make decisions about the urban landscape.

Nasaw was followed by Mark Hewitt, an architect and expert on Carrère and Hastings, who explained, in a calm but impassioned cadence, that when the 42nd Street Library was completed in 1911, it was viewed as "one of the technological wonders of America." In the 1890s, the NYPL's founder, Dr. Billings, toured the world's great libraries and conceived a bold idea that initially drew ridicule: to construct a grand Reading Room on top of seven levels of book stacks, whose contents would be delivered to readers in a small elevator. Those seven levels of book stacks, Hewitt explained, "are a marvel of early 20th-century engineering . . . and it will require an engineering marvel to dismantle them." Concluded Hewitt: "The logic behind the current plan completely escapes me."

The Q&A began with Marx's pointed riposte to Hewitt: "Yes, the stacks were a marvel of book preservation a hundred years ago. They are *not* a marvel of book preservation today." Darnton challenged Nasaw's assertion that the CLP was conceived "behind closed doors." "As a trustee," he said, "I've never seen a door closed. All meetings of the trustees are open to the public." (That is technically true, but Nasaw was right: when the trustees go into "executive session," in which the most consequential business is discussed, members of the public are expelled from the room and there is no record of the discussion in the minutes.)

Tension was building in the auditorium, but Darnton, turning to a fellow panelist, defused it: "I must say that of all the contributions this evening, that of Mark Hewitt takes me aback. A lot of your arguments were new to me. I haven't appreciated them. I think I need to consider them further. I don't think we, in any way, want to damage this building." But Darnton wasn't ready to capitulate to his critics: "The NYPL has a fundamental problem . . . we face a very extreme financial crisis."

Four months later, on September 19, 2012, the olive branch, which Marx had hinted at in the New School debate, appeared: the NYPL's trustees agreed to outfit a second level of bookshelves underneath Bryant Park. A wealthy trustee, Abby Milstein, pledged $8 million for the construction costs.

Marx hoped that this announcement would satisfy his critics and clear a path toward Foster's renovation. The Milstein gift prompted Darnton to write another essay for *The New York Review of Books* on October 25, 2012, hailing what he called "a turning point" in the NYPL debate. "These changes," he wrote, "should go a long way toward satisfying the desire of researchers to follow up leads and check references by consulting works that are stored a short distance from their desks." Darnton finished with these words:

> Plans are still being developed, and no doubt there will continue to be considerable disagreement about them. But the public debate has served the public well, and the debaters should know not only that they have been heard but also that they have had an effect in shaping the biggest change in the library since it opened 101 years ago.

A *New York Times* story called the Milstein gift "a significant shift in the Central Library Plan." But the decision to build another level of shelving under Bryant Park left the critics with a mouthful of ashes. They knew they had won a partial victory, but as Stanley Katz told the *Times* on September 19: "This doesn't respond almost at all to the fundamental critique of the Central Library Plan as it still exists." Katz's skepticism was entirely warranted: the new shelves under Bryant Park were not built.

The momentum belonged to the NYPL, and it seemed to library-watchers that, with this concession to the critics, the CLP was back on track. In an editorial, one of the city's tabloids, *The New York Daily News*, which is owned by the real-estate developer Mortimer Zuckerman and which had championed the Library plan from the beginning, wrote on September 23, 2012: "Marx can now confidently proceed with his bold renovation. As for the critics, they can shush."

The autumn of 2012 was a frustrating period for a group that came together in the spring and summer to exchange ideas on how to resist the CLP. The group included Scott and Katz; Crain and Petersen; Charles Warren and Mark Hewitt; Monica Strauss, a New York–based art historian; and Veronika Conant, a retired librarian from Hunter College who had conducted, with others, a tenacious campaign to save the Donnell Library. A pair of well-known authors also got involved: Annalyn Swan, who won a Pulitzer Prize in 2005 for her biography of Willem de Kooning (written with Mark Stevens), and David Levering Lewis, the NYU historian.

By late September, many of these critics were dejected—mainly because of the Milstein gift, which they feared would doom the old stacks at 42nd Street and hasten the demise of the Mid-Manhattan Library, but also because of the departure of Crain and Petersen from their ranks. Crain had largely retreated from the debate; he saw the Milstein gift as a significant compromise, and something of a victory for those concerned about the Library's research mission. He was also keen to return to writing assignments for which he might conceivably be paid. Petersen moved to Cambridge to begin a Ph.D. program in U.S. history at Harvard. (Despite the loss of Crain and Petersen, the group would, after many stops and starts, slowly coalesce into an anarchic but nevertheless effective activist organization.)

Moreover, the critics began to hear accusations of elitism that flowed directly from an op-ed piece, "Sacking a

Palace of Culture," that Edmund Morris, a Pulitzer Prize–winning author, had published in the *Times* in April 2012, a few weeks before the New School debate. Morris's essay, by turns elegiac and knife-like, was the work of an NYPL loyalist: he recalled the afternoon he sat next to Arthur Miller in the microfilm room at 42nd Street, and peeked over Miller's shoulder to see what he was reading. It was "an old news article about Marilyn Monroe."

For Morris, the CLP marked the demise of a once-great research institution. In dressing the corpse, he outlined the decay of the NYPL's Performing Arts Library at Lincoln Center, whose expert staff had been decimated through attrition and reassignment, and whose facility now "exudes a dispirited air of neglect. As Bette Davis must be on record growling somewhere in the archive (or in offsite storage), 'What a dump!'"

But the Lincoln Center facility wasn't always a dump. Indeed, in 1975, Morris had published, in the *Times*, a tribute to the Dance Collection, whose carpeted reading room "is something of a club for the dance fraternity: on any given day one may see Makarova researching the style of a predecessor, or Frederick Ashton thumbing through a few of his old programs, or Alvin Ailey refreshing his memory of an Alvin Ailey ballet." It was a paradise lost.

The first five paragraphs of Morris's 2012 *Times* essay were well expressed. But the piece jumped the rails in paragraph six: "Ominously, the aroma of the coffee bean already infuses the lovely vestibule [at 42nd Street] . . . There's much to be said for caffeine, but it attracts tourists like flies . . . And the marble floor nowadays is loud with the squeak of Reeboks." This language was a gift to Marx: for the next two years, he would use Morris's essay as a cudgel against the critics, none of whom shared Morris's clearly elitist views, but all of whom paid a price for his words.

A letter that Joan Scott e-mailed to a friend in October 2012 conveys the bleak mood of the critics in the months following the Milstein gift and the Morris op-ed:

> I may be a pessimist or a realist, but I think we've lost this one. Yes, there will be protests when (if ever) the Foster plans are revealed, but I don't think we have much traction on this anymore . . . Half of the signatories to my letter will buy the line that we have prevailed (the books on site being what really matters to them), and it will be very hard to rally a significant group of the others—so we will look like a small, pesky group of "elite" scholars who are trying to stop "progress" rather than serious New Yorkers (and their fellow library users) trying to save a major institution for the public good . . . The forces of capital have beat us on this one.

Scott, it turned out, was too gloomy. Influential figures in the press were investigating Foster's renovation, and their findings would neatly complement her own views of the situation at the NYPL.

•

When Ada Louise Huxtable published her piece on the advent of the Jefferson Market Library in Greenwich Village in 1964, she had been the *Times*' architecture critic for a year. Indeed, Huxtable was the first full-time architecture critic ever hired by an American newspaper, and she was already known for her clear, distinctive voice. When New York's Penn Station was destroyed, she wrote on May 5, 1963: "It's time we stopped talking about our affluent society. We are an impoverished society. It is a poor society indeed that can't pay for these amenities; that has no money for anything except expressways to rush people out of our dull and deteriorating cities."

Huxtable, who was awarded a Pulitzer Prize in 1970, championed historic preservation and cities built on a human scale; she loathed the corruption of architecture by money, and the excesses of commercial development. "I wish people would stop asking me what my favorite buildings are," she wrote in 1971. "I do not think it really matters very much what my personal favorites are, except as they illuminate principles of design and execution useful and essential to the collective spirit that we call society. For irreplaceable examples of that spirit I will do real battle."

When the controversy began, Huxtable was ninety-one and in failing health. She had left the *Times* in 1997 to become the architecture critic of *The Wall Street Journal*. Though she wrote less frequently, her voice was still distinctive and battle-ready. When she began a deep investigation of the CLP in the summer of 2012, she encountered silence: three phone calls she made to the NYPL were ignored until a high-ranking City official intervened on her behalf. The NYPL finally responded to Huxtable and promised her schematics of Foster's design by September 2012, a date that came and went. By November, Huxtable still didn't have the NYPL's design, and she believed that crucial details were being withheld from her. She went ahead and wrote up her findings. Her essay, "Undertaking Its Destruction," appeared in *The Wall Street Journal* on December 3, 2012.

It was a thunderbolt. "There is no more important landmark building in New York than the New York Public Library," she began, "yet it is about to undertake its own destruction." Huxtable had followed the debate with care, and she was the first to point out that "the stacks are the structural support of the [Rose] reading room. They literally hold it up." The NYPL's structural engineer would soon tell *The Wall Street Journal* that the removal of the stacks would be like "cutting the legs off a table while dinner is being served."

Moreover, she alerted her readers to the underlying architectural logic of the building: "All of Carrère and Hastings' elegant classicism is not just window dressing. Their wonderful spatial relationships and rich detail are intimately tied to the building's remarkable functional rationale."

NYPL officials had told Huxtable that the renovation was imperative because of a 41 percent decrease in the use of the collections over the last fifteen years, and that only 6 percent of print sources were consulted every year. (Staff members question those statistics.) But she felt those figures were "misleading":

> A research library is devoted to the acquisition, maintenance and availability of collections of amazing range, rarity and depth, much of which will not be consulted for decades, have not been digitized and probably never will be. If we could estimate how many ways in which the world has been changed by that 6%, the number would be far more meaningful than the traffic through its lion-guarded doors . . . a research library is a timeless repository of treasures, not a popularity contest measured by head counts, the current arbiter of success. This is already the most democratic of institutions, free and open to all. Democracy and populism seem to have become hopelessly confused.

Huxtable's reporting and research led her to this conclusion: "This is a plan devised out of a profound ignorance . . . you don't 'update' a masterpiece." To the NYPL's brass she made the following recommendation: "Keep the Mid-Manhattan building; the location is perfect. Let Foster+Partners loose on the Mid-Manhattan building: the results will be spectacular, and probably no more costly than the extravagant and destructive plan the library has chosen."

"Undertaking Its Destruction" was Huxtable's final essay: she died a month later. A few weeks after her death, twenty prominent architecture writers, critics, and historians signed a letter to Marx assailing Foster's renovation. They called their endeavor the "Huxtable Initiative."

On December 19, 2012, Foster presented his design, which featured an atrium with a curved staircase, at a crowded press conference at 42nd Street. The press release given to reporters promised a "modern, light-filled" circulating library "with views of Bryant Park." During the Q&A, I asked Foster if he had any misgivings in light of Huxtable's cri de coeur two weeks earlier. "No," he replied. "The history of the building is one of change over time."

The next question came from Caleb Crain, who observed that one feature was missing from the schematic design: the mechanism to bring books from the shelves under Bryant Park into the Rose Reading Room. Marx, who shared the podium with Foster, offered a vague reply. Charles Warren, the architect, pressed Marx on the point. Afterward, Foster approached Warren and remarked that the books would be brought to the Rose Reading Room on a conveyor system "just like baggage in an airport." Warren asked Foster if books ought to be treated like baggage, and told him that he was on the cusp of destroying "the most elegantly engineered system of book storage and delivery ever devised." Foster held his tongue and walked away.

Foster's plan did not impress the architecture critics, either. "NOT GOOD ENOUGH," was the headline of Mark

Lamster's review in *Design Observer*, which said that the plan resembled "a bloated Barnes & Noble." "Unfortunately," wrote James S. Russell of *Bloomberg Business*, "the Foster design proffers graceless skinny columns rising through the atrium to a flimsy looking parasol-shaped ceiling." For Russell, it was "thin architectural gruel."

The New York Times waited more than five weeks to comment. On January 29, 2013, Michael Kimmelman, now the paper's architecture critic, produced his assessment, which appeared on page one of the print edition. After extensive reporting, Kimmelman wrote: "I'm not buying it." He went on to explain why he couldn't endorse a scheme that would allow Foster to turn the 42nd Street Library into "a guinea pig"; that was "a potential Alamo of engineering, architecture and finance"; and whose financial underpinnings were opaque. He got Marx to admit that the "cost may rise to $340 or $350 million" and asked for a "detailed cost analysis" by at least one independent party—"not one of the firms the library has already hired."

It was an unusually robust intervention in a newspaper that had always championed the NYPL, but Kimmelman was already carving out a distinctive voice, with far more interest in urbanism than his predecessor, Nicolai Ouroussoff. A battle-scarred historic preservationist remarked to me that Kimmelman's essay was the most striking piece of architecture criticism the *Times* had published in decades. In his final paragraph, Kimmelman advised the NYPL's trustees to chart a new course: "The last thing they'd want to be remembered for is trashing their landmark building and digging a money pit."

Kimmelman's spirited commentary did not go unanswered. In a letter to the *Times*, Foster condemned the essay as a "diatribe" and insisted that "the option of doing nothing with the book stacks does not exist; they do not comply with current fire safety codes or book conservation standards." As for the financial outlay for the project, Foster wrote: "There is no inherent risk of cost overruns."

A second letter to the *Times* from Marx hailed the CLP as "financially prudent" and "wonderfully ambitious." "The Central Library Plan has been the subject of public discussion for five years," Marx wrote. "Waiting is not an option."

6

"I Will Raise the Money"

On January 30, 2013, Charles Warren, the architect who had accosted Norman Foster at the press conference six weeks earlier, gave a lecture titled "Keeping the Stacks Intact." It took place around the corner from the 42nd Street Library, in one of Manhattan's overlooked gems: the atmospheric library of the General Society of Mechanics and Tradesmen, at 20 West 44th Street, the second-oldest library in the city.

A number of historic preservationists, library stalwarts, and community activists had turned up to hear Warren speak. There were few empty seats. Kimmelman's front-page *Times* essay had appeared the day before, and many of those in attendance had read it carefully.

Scrupulous in his attire, Warren, sixty-one, rarely leaves his apartment on West 101st Street without a jacket and tie. Throughout his career, he has balanced an active architecture practice with scholarship, and Warren is not the kind of man who brandishes leaflets and walks picket lines. Indeed, he hadn't protested anything since the Vietnam War. But with this lecture, he was headed into unfamiliar terrain: the threat to the 42nd Street Library had pushed him toward activism.

His friends affirm that he is a force to be reckoned with. Says Robert A. M. Stern: "Charles Warren is very talented, intelligent, and knowledgeable—traits that are rarely combined in an architect. Possessed of a healthy cynicism, a sly wit, a passion to do good work, he flies just beneath the radar of New York's establishment, which is just fine because it enables him to get things done while the chattering classes drone on."

Warren's lecture concerned not only the "beauty and clarity" of the 42d Street Library—qualities, he said, that are "conceptual as well as visual"—but also the reasons why the building is "a perfect machine for reading, storing, and caring for books." He offered a brisk overview of the book stacks: "a dense hive of cast-iron shelves, which is hung from 1,300 thin steel columns." The hive contains 98,000 adjustable and 16,000 fixed shelves, encased within columns built in part with Carnegie steel. (The word "CARNEGIE" can be seen at the top of certain columns.) As Warren explained:

> Remarkably, this system also supports the floor of the magnificent Rose Reading Room above. These

> construction innovations were granted U.S. patents, and the Library's spatial organization is equally ingenious. A lift rises through the tiers of shelves, delivering requested books to the center of the main reading room. That room itself, 297 by 78 feet, is a grandly proportioned space at the end of an almost operatic procession that visitors take via marble staircases ascending from the main entrance. On other levels, lavishly paneled rooms surround the stacks on three sides. The choreography of readers and books is central to the building's architectural experience.

Now it was under threat. "Foster," said Warren, "would consign the elegant iron-and-steel structure at the building's center to the ash heap of history." It was a scheme, he said, that "destroys the efficient, axial poetry of Carrère & Hastings, replacing the stacks with disconnected elements from elsewhere. The atmosphere reminds us of Foster's London Stansted Airport, and the stair belongs to his ill-fated Harmon Hotel at Las Vegas's CityCenter. The railings and soffits look like grilles on the latest Lincoln MKZ."

Not every NYPL critic was persuaded by Warren's argument that the stacks are integral to the Library's mission. "As for the stacks, I never had any romantic attachment to the physical structure itself," says Charles Petersen of *n+1*. "I really could not care less whether there are books in there or not." Petersen's principal concern was the loss of the NYPL's research capacity.

At the end of the lecture, Paula Glatzer, an independent Shakespeare scholar, raised her hand and asked if there was any organized resistance to the CLP. Aside from the journalistic writings of Caleb Crain and Charles Petersen, Warren replied, not much was happening by way of activism. At which point, Crain, who was in the audience, stood up and remarked, with a touch of despair and self-deprecation: "Don't expect us to do anything, we're journalists and writers!"—a quip that generated laughter. (Crain was never comfortable with an activist approach to the NYPL's difficulties.) As the event broke up, people stood around in groups, anxiously exchanging information and considering possible next steps. Animated conversations spilled out onto West 44th Street.

"The event felt like a breakthrough," Warren told me later. For much of the previous year, 2012, the formless group of critics had virtually no traction, and little notion of how to organize; they felt isolated. But, to their delight, Huxtable and Kimmelman had just savaged the underlying rationale for the CLP, and other leading architecture critics had damned Foster's design. Warren's lecture was the first time that all the critics had found themselves under one roof, in an emotionally charged atmosphere. "I was surprised," Warren told me, "by the forceful, pointed response of the audience—they were demanding action, apparently from me."

•

But time was short. The Foster renovation had been fast-tracked, and the NYPL's core trustees were steely and assured—and not unduly concerned about Huxtable's *Wall Street Journal* essay, or the dismal reviews of Foster's design. Nor, it seems, did they take seriously the critics' argument that installing a new climate-control system in the stacks would be much cheaper than destroying them. Still, they sensed that complications lay ahead. "While public response generally has been positive to the visuals by [Foster] that were released in December of 2012," the trustee-meeting minutes of January 23, 2013, state, "the project is not free from controversy and some further negative reviews should be anticipated." (Indeed, Kimmelman's essay would appear six days later.)

By way of regulatory review, Mayor Bloomberg and the City Council had cleared a smooth path for the renovation. Marx had to navigate only one procedural hurdle: the New York City Landmarks Preservation Commission.

As part of its application to that agency, however, the Library had to seek approval from Manhattan's Community Board 5. In the city's political landscape, community boards can function, to a limited extent, as a bulwark against elite power, and the NYPL came prepared to the CB5 meeting on January 17, 2013. Marx showed up with half a dozen colleagues, and with several well-dressed young men from Foster's office, who, with their crisp English accents, described the architect's vision.

Drama ensued when Marx began to speak: as he outlined

the virtues of the renovation, a waggish, dark-haired young man in a corner interrupted him with an insouciant question—"*So when is Starbucks coming?*" This was salt in the wound: in 2012, Anthony T. Grafton, a celebrated historian and library expert at Princeton University, had written in *The Daily Princetonian*, "My stomach hurts when I think about NYPL, the first great library I ever worked in, turned into a vast internet café, where people can read the same Google Books that they could access at home or from Starbucks."

At the mention of Starbucks, Marx lost his cool and proceeded to berate the young man for two minutes straight: the coffee chain, Marx shouted, doesn't possess imperishable manuscripts by Beethoven, Whitman, and Joyce, along with millions of books and rare manuscripts, all of which are freely accessible to the public; nor does Starbucks operate ninety libraries in New York City. CB5 accepted his arguments, and voted 33 to 1 to approve a resolution endorsing the CLP. Documents obtained under the Freedom of Information Law show that CB5's resolution was a near replica of talking points provided by the NYPL's busy public relations office. (The NYPL ignored all of my FOIL requests.)

The Landmarks Preservation Commission—controlled by Bloomberg appointees—turned out to be an easy hurdle to clear. The Carrère and Hastings stacks were never landmarked, and the NYPL went before the commission to request just a handful of minor alterations to the building's exterior. At a public hearing on January 22, 2013, which occurred a week before Kimmelman's page-one essay appeared, activists spoke passionately in defense of the stacks and against the Foster plan; but the majority of the LPC commissioners already knew where they stood. The event had a scripted quality.

By a vote of 6–2, in a drab meeting room inside the forty-story Municipal Building, the LPC's board approved the NYPL's application—a decision that amounted to a decisive green light for the CLP; the NYPL celebrated with a press release.

The rubber stamp from the Landmarks Preservation Commission in January 2013—combined with COO Offensend's declaration a month later, at a trustee meeting, that construction at 42nd Street would begin almost immediately—sent a chill through the critics, and lent credence to a disconcerting message they'd received months earlier from an unnamed but seemingly well-informed and sympathetic insider at the NYPL. This person, whose message was delivered by a third party, said it was "doubtful" that arguments from the critics would have any useful effect on the trustees: "The real-estate people on the board see all of this as a great game, an opportunity that is about real estate—not about content or the serious purpose of a library."

Marx, the insider observed, was very close to victory: "The only way the Library plan is going to get derailed is if the City of New York does not chip in the $150 million that has been promised. If politics intrudes and that money is cut or withdrawn, then the plan is likely to collapse."

•

Organizing against the NYPL turned out to be harder than Charles Warren had anticipated. "I had thought," he says, "that some preservation organization would just take up the issue." The likely candidate to step forward was the Municipal Art Society (MAS), for decades the loudest voice for historic preservation in New York City. But MAS had filled its board with trustees from the real-estate and business sectors, and had retreated significantly from activism.

Fortunately for Warren, one nonprofit organization with a broad ambit was in a combative mood: the Historic Districts Council (HDC), led by Simeon Bankoff, forty-four, a dyed-in-the-wool New Yorker and maverick. HDC, which is located in the former rectory of the St. Mark's Church-in-the-Bowery, has been around since 1970 and, in recent years, has supplanted MAS as the most fearless, energetic, and fleet-footed historic preservationist outfit in New York. Bankoff was aware of what was happening at the Library: his friend Zack Winestine, an NYPL activist, had been feeding him regular updates.

In a written statement in March 2013, HDC affirmed: "The New York Public Library is arguably a nearly perfect design for uniting New Yorkers with knowledge in much the same way that Grand Central Terminal is a nearly perfect design for uniting New Yorkers with transportation." The CLP, HDC declared, was "a real-estate deal conceived to maximize profits through decreasing services," and a scheme that will "eviscerate the heart of the 42nd Street Library."

The critics had found a valuable ally: in early 2013, HDC helped to create an organizational structure for the work that the activists were trying, with greater intensity but still limited success, to do on their own. In May 2013, under HDC's tutelage, a nonprofit organization was formed: The Committee to Save the New York Public Library (CSNYPL), whose meetings took place at HDC's office.

Charles Warren became the president; the vice president was Theodore Grunewald, an architect by training, who had testified at the January Landmarks hearing. Grunewald cannot be missed in a crowd: he has short brown hair and a long beard, and he favors plaid and striped seersucker, wool, and tweed suits, worn with a vest and his grandfather's pocket watch on a silver chain. The only things missing are the monocle and the walking stick. "A cross between William Morris and Allen Ginsberg," is how Caleb Crain described Grunewald's attire the night of Warren's lecture.

But Grunewald is not a fop, dandy, or curio: he's an indefatigable activist who devotes his time to the preservation of exquisite New York buildings and public spaces. He can often be found at Gene's, an old-fashioned Italian eatery whose décor evokes the old New York of Joseph Mitchell. But he will also be the first to sacrifice a perfect springtime Sunday afternoon to remain indoors crafting handmade signs for demonstrations—which would soon take place, on a regular basis starting in spring 2013, at the Fifth Avenue entrance of the Library.

Warren and Grunewald were an odd couple: Warren's

temperament favored subtle diplomacy, whereas Grunewald's method was rough-edged and confrontational. But they found a way to get along and advance the work of their little group, which had grown to include about twenty-five people, including the core group that came together around the time of the New School debate, and which continued to work informally all through 2012, spreading news of the CLP through their own networks. Now they had their own nonprofit organization, whose primary message reprised Huxtable's critique: renovate the stacks, don't demolish them; and transform the Mid-Manhattan into a vibrant, first-rate library. As the CSNYPL became more efficient in the summer of 2013, its members realized, as Bloomberg prepared to leave office, that their overriding goal must be to stop the clock and delay the CLP until a new mayor was elected.

A third crucial member of the CSNYPL was Zack Winestine. While taking time off from Princeton University, Winestine, who sports a scruffy beard and stylish round glasses, got a job as the assistant to the director of photography on Stanley Kubrick's *The Shining*. He went on to be a camera assistant for movies, including *Crocodile Dundee* and *Ironweed*, and later produced and directed several independent films. (He has also shot music videos for the B-52s, ZZ Top, and Public Enemy.) In 2000, during protests in Washington, D.C., against the World Bank and the International Monetary Fund, he was arrested in an act of civil disobedience, after which he spent five days in the D.C.

Federal Penitentiary. For several years, using the NYPL's workrooms, he's been writing a book about European fascism and the avant-garde.

Winestine had closely followed the controversy from the outset. But he waited a year before hurling himself into the campaign. In a January 2013 e-mail introducing himself to Katz and Scott, Winestine wrote: "I've been an avid user of the 42nd Street Library since grade school, and consider it in many ways to be the *omphalos* of the city." It was Winestine who would create the infrastructure that made the campaign possible: he assembled and managed the CSNYPL website (savenypl.org), Facebook page, and e-mail announcement list; he wrote leaflets and press releases for the rallies, at which he was the liaison to the police; and he performed sophisticated research on various facets of the campaign. Winestine became so essential to the CSNYPL that, when frustration and exhaustion led him to withdraw for several months in late 2013, there was near-panic in the ranks.

Other CSNYPL members and fellow travelers included Scott and Katz; Glatzer, the Shakespeare scholar from Warren's lecture, who would spend dozens of hours reaching out to elected officials; Annalyn Swan, who (with Mark Stevens) owed Alfred A. Knopf a biography of Francis Bacon, but found time for NYPL action; Simon Verity, a sculptor and master stonecutter whose pieces have been acquired by Elton John and the Prince of Wales; Elizabeth A. R. Brown, a medieval historian; Monica Strauss, the art historian; Veronika Conant, the retired librarian who tried to save the Donnell; and Michael White and Carolyn McIntyre, who formed their own organization, Citizens Defending Libraries, which worked closely with the CSNYPL.

Spring 2013 saw the deepening involvement of *Times* architecture critic Michael Kimmelman. The NYPL renovation had gotten under his skin, and that meant trouble for Marx and the trustees. Wavy-haired and quietly charismatic, Kimmelman, who was born to activist parents in Greenwich Village, is a formidable journalistic presence. Kenneth Tynan, the acclaimed British theater critic, kept a message above his writing desk: "Be light, stinging, insolent and melancholy." Kimmelman's writing has all of those qualities (minus the insolence), but he also brings to the critic's job the virtues of a diligent and detail-oriented beat reporter. After serving as both the chief art critic and a Berlin-based columnist for the *Times*, Kimmelman, who also performs as a pianist, returned to New York in 2011 and, to a large extent, reinvented the architecture beat at the *Times*, infusing it with the spirit of Jane Jacobs.

"Kimmelman is the best architecture critic since Ada Louise Huxtable and definitely the first one since her who has looked at New York City from an urban perspective rather than simply following architectural trends and fads," says HDC's Simeon Bankoff. "Kimmelman actually talks about the role of architecture in civic life rather than the buildings as an object."

In early 2013, after publishing his front-page essay on the Foster renovation, Kimmelman brought the NYPL controversy into his regular reviews and columns. In March, chance offered him the opportunity to write about two historic libraries in Paris—the Bibliothèque Ste.-Geneviève and the Bibliothèque nationale, both designed by Henri Labrouste (1801–1875), who was the subject of a new exhibition at the Museum of Modern Art titled "Henri Labrouste: Structure Brought to Light." In his review of the show, Kimmelman noted:

> The exhibition's arrival seems almost uncanny in the midst of the debate over the renovation of Carrère and Hastings' New York Public Library building at 42nd Street, whose iron book stacks derive from Labrouste's. Library officials have proposed removing those historic stacks . . . [which] they say are too dilapidated and unsuited to be modernized. But Labrouste's even-older stacks at the Bibliothèque nationale have recently been outfitted with modern climate controls and fireproofing and will be opened to the reading public. The exhibition's last room greets visitors with a large photomural of that space—a pointed rebuke to those New York library officials who haven't adequately justified their scheme and might now want to investigate more closely what Paris is doing.

Kimmelman also used Twitter to comment on events. In early May 2013, after Marx unveiled his plans for a refurbished Donnell Library at the base of the luxury tower, Kimmelman tweeted: "Further NYPL tales: plans unveiled for far smaller Donnell, in hotel basement, its stress on bleacher seating." (The old Donnell was 97,000 square feet; the new one will be 28,000 square feet.) A few days later, after the trustees authorized a $9 million payment to Norman Foster, he tweeted: "NYPL spending millions of tax $$ on plan to gut 42nd St. stacks, despite lack of design, budget, public support."

Kimmelman homed in on the question of public support. "Asked @NYPL to be put in touch with supporters of Central Library plan for 42nd St. Haven't met any. No word from Library. You out there?" he tweeted on May 13. And in June, *New York* magazine published a profile of Kimmelman titled "The People's Critic," in which he clarified the stakes of the NYPL engagement: "If you're going to be spending untold millions on this plan, it better be what the city really, really needs. Otherwise, this will be considered one of the calamities of the city's history, along with Penn Station."

Meanwhile, fast-moving developments at 42nd Street sent a shudder through the CSNYPL. In March 2013, its members learned that three million books had been, over a twelve-month period, quietly removed from the old stacks under the Rose Reading Room. Many of them wound up in the possession of a private storage company. Now the dense hive was ghostly, and the building's heart emitted a dank stench: the climate-control system in the stacks had been turned off after the last book was sent away. Staff members say that large numbers of books and photographs were damaged when the stacks were emptied, a claim that NYPL officials deny. Around this time, the activists also learned that the penthouse in the luxury tower that had replaced the Donnell was on the market for $60 million. That the NYPL had received $59 million for the entire property fueled their suspicions that it had been undersold.

COO Offensend had said that construction would begin almost immediately, which prompted the activists to closely monitor the website of the NYC Buildings Department, waiting for the official permits to be issued. On June 1, Winestine sent an e-mail to his group's internal listserv: "Dear Friends: Seven new Department of Buildings permits have just appeared for 471 Fifth Avenue (the street address for the 42nd Street Library). All are dated May 31, 2013. Unfortunately, I think these may be the permits we have been waiting for."

Three days later, at a City Council library hearing, Christabel Gough, a volunteer historic preservationist of stately bearing, confronted Marx with printouts of the permits. "I see you have your permits to start demolition," she said. Marx, who was taken aback, told Gough there was nothing to worry about, and referred her to a colleague across the room, Joanna Pestka, the NYPL's vice president for planning and construction. Pestka looked at Gough's printouts and remarked dismissively: "Oh, those."

•

The dispute finally entered the realm of politics after Micah Kellner, a thirty-four-year-old member of the State Assembly, seized the issue. Kellner was not well known—few people in New York City follow politics in Albany, the state capital—but he was shrewd and persistent; Eleuteria Slater, a longtime activist and a member of the CSNYPL who lived in his district, had alerted him to the urgency of the NYPL situation.

In spring of 2013, Kellner, who chaired the Assembly's library committee, began to look into the NYPL matter, and was given a tour of the empty stacks at 42nd Street. What he heard from Library executives left him disconcerted. He decided to call a public hearing, which took place on June 27, 2013, in City Council chambers across from City Hall, and was titled "The Sale of Public Libraries in New York City." Marx and his entourage showed up to find a full room, and Marx's aides—including his lieutenant, Offensend—began to pace nervously. It would be an eight-hour hearing, with testimony from fifty people.

When Marx began to speak, there was worry on his face. He rose from his chair to consult a nearby chart, but Assemblyman Kellner pointedly ordered him back to his seat. For fifteen minutes, Marx spoke in general terms about the NYPL, and then launched into a seven-minute explanation of the CLP. Time slowed down; audience members checked their phones and stifled yawns. But suddenly Marx raised his voice and deviated from his written text: "*I have heard the criticism*," he said, and pledged that the NYPL would provide what Kimmelman had demanded five months earlier: an independent cost analysis for the Foster renovation, as well as the price of some alternatives to it. Then, startingly, Marx said that the design Foster presented in December 2012 "was never meant to be a design."

Assemblyman Kellner leaned forward and asked Marx the first of a dozen questions: "*If we don't have a design yet, and we don't have a cost, why has the NYPL applied for and been granted building permits?*" Applause rang out from the audience. "Mr. Chairman," Marx replied, "those permits were for preliminary or preparatory work. We have *not* applied for a building permit to begin any demolition work in the stacks, and we will *not* apply for such permits until we have a plan and have made it public." *Times* reporter Robin Pogrebin was at the hearing, and her story the next day was headlined: "Critics Prompt New Review of Library Plan." (In December 2013, Kellner was censured by the New York State Assembly following allegations of sexual harassment, which he says were the result of a witch hunt unleashed by the speaker of the chamber, Sheldon Silver, who was himself arrested on corruption charges in early 2015. Kellner no longer serves in the Assembly.)

The discovery of the construction permits, combined with the Kellner hearing, were galvanizing events that gave rise to a pair of lawsuits in New York State Supreme Court in July 2013, the goal of which was to halt the renovation. The NYPL's sixty trustees were named in the lawsuits. The plaintiffs in the first lawsuit included Joan Scott, Stanley Katz, David Nasaw, Edmund Morris, and Annalyn Swan. A pugnacious Manhattan lawyer, Michael Hiller, accepted the case; his fee—$100,000—was paid for by Gough, the historic preservationist who confronted Marx with the permits, and who later said, "It was worth every penny."

The second lawsuit was initiated by NYU historian David Levering Lewis. Lewis, who was born in 1936, is grave, formal, carefully spoken, and thoroughly old-fashioned. He's an enormously productive and distinguished scholar who has written books about the Dreyfus Affair, Harlem, W.E.B. DuBois, Martin Luther King Jr., and African resistance to European imperialism. By and large, those books were researched and written in the Library of Congress and the New York Public Library, both of which Lewis cherished.

Lewis and Marx knew each other. Prior to the controversy, their relationship, says Lewis, was "distantly congenial" and "mutually admiring." Indeed, one of Marx's books had sparked an intuition that helped Lewis conceptualize a 2008 book, *God's Crucible: Islam and the Making of Europe, 570–1215*. When it was published, Lewis sent Marx an inscribed copy; Marx responded from Amherst with a cordial, handwritten letter.

Just a few hours after Marx read Lewis's remarks in my 2011 *Nation* story, he e-mailed him: "Hi David. Hope this finds you well. Meanwhile, we are enjoying beautiful bookshelves at home built by the person you suggested . . . I was wondering if we might get together at some point to catch up and to talk about the future of the Library (including this building—I heard you!)." But Lewis was not in an amiable mood, and he replied: "Maybe we should . . . confer with Sir Norman [Foster] about bookshelves."

They met for breakfast at the Metro Diner on 100th Street. Marx told Lewis, as he had recently told others, that the 42nd Street Library was intimidating to much of the public (younger people, the new immigrants) and had to be transformed and modernized. Marx then spoke feelingly of his boyhood in the NYPL branch libraries, and his desire to invigorate those facilities. Lewis asked where the money for the branches would come from, if $300 million was about to be spent on an extravagant architectural project at one facility—42nd Street. "I will raise the money," Marx said. "I can do it." "You are deceiving yourself," Lewis replied.

In January 2013, Lewis again conveyed his views to Marx via e-mail: "Greetings Tony. An inconvenient truth: the specter of Penn Station hovers over your CLP . . . Happy New Year, David." Marx wrote back immediately: "I hear you. I am not sure the Penn Station is a fair analogy as that building tragically is all gone and ours will remain, with double the public usage. But again, I hear you."

They stayed in touch. In May 2013, Lewis, in an e-mail, complained to Marx that scholarly services would erode under the CLP, and likened Foster's design to a suburban mall. Marx riposted: "I really object to the notion of a great circulating library as a mall. That seems rather elitist to me."

David Levering Lewis was finished with e-mail; it was

time to find a lawyer. Seven weeks later he and two friends, the community activist Jacob Morris and the book publisher John Macrae of Henry Holt and Company, took legal action to stop the Foster renovation. Lewis desired his own lawsuit, and so there were two well-publicized legal filings. The critics had aimed to stop the clock and buy time; the strategy worked. In early July 2013, days after Lewis filed his lawsuit, a judge issued a temporary restraining order. It read: "NYPL shall not undertake and/or continue any construction work . . . relating to the seven stories of iron-and-steel book stacks . . ."

7

"Don't Gut Our Lions"

Early in July 2013, an aide to Bill de Blasio, who was campaigning energetically for mayor, contacted library activist Michael White with a request: could he, in forty-eight hours, organize a rally in front of the 42nd Street landmark, at which the candidate would appear? White was delighted to oblige. On July 12, de Blasio, the City's public advocate, delivered a short speech on the Library steps, surrounded by thirty people holding signs that read: "GUT JOB," "CIVILIZATION DEMANDS LIBRARIES," and "I MISS MY 'KINDRED SPIRITS.'"

"These plans," de Blasio told the assembled, "seemed to have been made without any forethought to the building's historical and cultural integrity." As the crowd cheered, he demanded both the retention of the Mid-Manhattan Library and a "thorough, independent cost audit" of Foster's

$300 million renovation. The event was over quickly, as de Blasio raced to his next appointment; it was just another day on the campaign trail. But Foster's renovation had now been injected into the mayoral race. The next day's *Times* carried an item about the candidate's appearance on the Library steps, in which Neil Rudenstine, the chairman of the NYPL's board, said: "This plan will generate funding to provide more books, librarians, and programs."

It wasn't the first, or the last, demonstration in front of the 42nd Street Library: the CSNYPL had begun to picket the trustee meetings. The rallies were never large—rarely more than one hundred people showed up—but they were well organized. On several occasions the protestors were joined by the activist Reverend Billy Talen (a faux clergyman) and his choir, who provided a loud musical backdrop to the proceedings.

The events were not without their moments of drama: expensively attired trustees were subjected to pointed questions on their way to and from their meeting room, in which chants were audible. At a rally on June 4, 2013, one trustee, Henry Louis Gates Jr., the esteemed Harvard professor, walked past the lions and noticed the protestors. A performer from Reverend Billy's choir who calls herself Dragonfly shouted at him: "Brother Gates!" He turned his head and smiled. At which point she unleashed a piercing volley of abuse: "Don't you know that closing the libraries will really affect our communities of color! Where will they go after school when they have *no* after-school programs to go to?" Gates kept walking and silently mounted the steps of the Library. (Three months later, I had a strange encounter with Gates. When he entered the branch library at 136th Street for a trustee meeting, I introduced myself and asked him, in the lobby, for his thoughts on the CLP. He glared at me, leaned over, and whispered into my ear: "*You don't want any trouble, do you, guy?*" Then, with a beaming smile, he turned his back and greeted his fellow trustees.)

The Wall Street Journal and the city's tabloids were now beginning to chronicle NYPL's tensions. On July 8, 2013, the *New York Post*—which, unlike its rival, *The New York Daily News*, had never supported the renovation on its editorial page—published a scalding essay by Nicole Gelinas, a contributing editor of *City Journal*, the magazine of the conservative Manhattan Institute. In contrast to the gracefully written essays by Huxtable and Kimmelman, Gelinas's article, "Real-Estate Fiction: NY Public Library's Risky Scheme," had a raw, elbow-in-the-face quality. But it wasn't hackwork: Gelinas had sat through Kellner's hearing and had done her own reporting on the minutiae of the CLP. (Another Manhattan Institute fellow, Stephen Eide, spent months in 2013 investigating the CLP, and came out against it in a long essay in *City Journal*.)

"Last week," Gelinas wrote, "a group of professors and historians filed suit against the New York Public Library, alleging that the library board's plan to demolish its book 'stacks' at 42nd Street violates its mission to protect books. But the plan could be a *fiscal* disaster, too—making the NYPL the latest institution to go broke thanks to vanity real estate."

Apropos of the Donnell Library, Gelinas highlighted the "tired excuses" Marx had offered at the Kellner hearing—at which the NYPL's leader blamed the 2008 recession for the collapse of the Orient-Express deal and implied that the Library wasn't responsible for the debacle—and noted the risk inherent in the CLP:

> Envision this, then: The nightmare scenario is that *after* the NYPL has sold off its prime real estate to another savvy developer, the library will become embroiled in a nightmare project on 42nd Street that costs multiples of today's estimate and takes a decade instead of five years. The library is doing this because it says it *needs* money (go figure).

When I asked Chairman Rudenstine for his rejoinder to Gelinas's essay and Michael Kimmelman's latest round of tweets, his reply was brief. "I don't follow Twitter," he said, "and do not read the *New York Post*."

But other NYPL trustees were closely following the controversy, and were shaken by the rush of events. "I am a true believer in the CLP," Robert Darnton told me in August 2013. "It's the best way to address the very serious financial problem" at the NYPL. But he added that he had been "rocked, worried" by Huxtable's *Wall Street Journal* essay. His own view of Foster's design—which, he revealed, had been "withdrawn"—was this: "It just didn't set my imagination on fire." Any future design by the British architect for the 42nd Street building, Darnton maintained, "should be architecturally superb. Anything less than excellent isn't adequate."

Meanwhile, Marx and the trustees on his executive committee—the NYPL's highest leadership body, which didn't include Darnton—embarked on a strategy to break ground on the project while Bloomberg was still in charge of the city. At the Kellner hearing and in other public venues, Marx had conveyed the impression that Foster's scheme was under reconsideration—that the design "was never meant to be a design." But on August 27, 2013, the NYPL inked a three-month, $25,000 contract with an influential lobbying and public relations firm, the Parkside Group, a decision that reflected the determination of the NYPL's leadership to move forward. "The renovation of the Central Library is urgently needed and is crucial to the success of NYPL," COO Offensend wrote in late August in an affidavit for David Levering Lewis's lawsuit. "NYPL has estimated that a six-month delay in its ability to implement the CLP would result in an escalation of costs of approximately 2%, which would likely translate to a loss of many millions of dollars for NYPL."

Marx's contract with Parkside, a copy of which was leaked to the *Times*, stipulated a "principal overarching goal: identifying potential supporters that can help the Library build support for the renovation plan." The shock troops would include construction unions: the "Mason Tenders District of

LIUNA . . . NYC District Council of Carpenters . . . Teamsters Joint Council 16." Parkside not only promised to recruit "PTAs, clergy, and leaders of immigrant organizations" to the pro-NYPL faction, but also to help Marx and his team "refine its materials and talking points."

The decision to hire Parkside coincided with an unexpected turn in the mayor's race: the candidate who had addressed a few dozen people on the steps of the Library in July, Bill de Blasio, was surging ahead of Christine Quinn, the City Council speaker and the presumed front-runner in the Democratic primary. Quinn was an advocate of Foster's renovation; the Council, under her leadership, promised $15 million to the CLP in 2011, which formed part of the $150 million allocated to the Library that year.

Three weeks before election day, Kimmelman published a to-do list for the next mayor in the *Times,* in which he called for a rethinking of some "undercooked Bloomberg initiatives"—i.e., "awarding $150 million in taxpayer money to redo the New York Public Library building at 42nd Street before there was even a solid renovation plan."

Fortified by the support from Kimmelman, Assemblyman Kellner, the *New York Post*, and Bill de Blasio, the CSNYPL was emboldened to picket the NYPL's annual fund-raising dinner on November 4, 2013, a day before de Blasio easily beat his Republican rival. This was a maneuver aimed at the Library's soft underbelly: the Library Lions dinner is a significant event in Manhattan society, and a lucrative fund-raising occasion for the NYPL. The honorees and guests included Henry Kissinger, Graydon Carter, Allison Rockefeller, Katherine Boo, Jonathan Franzen, Oscar and Annette de la Renta, Stephen Sondheim, Zadie Smith, Junot Díaz, and Mayor Bloomberg.

"Blocked from entering the party by the New York Police Department," *The Wall Street Journal* reported, the protestors "chatted up note-taking journalists, handed out fliers and chanted: 'Save our stacks!'" The *Journal* noted that when Stephen Schwarzman walked past the demonstrators, a friend of the financier's remarked to him: "Don't worry, none of them are from Blackstone!"—a quip that made Schwarzman smile.

The CSNYPL, many of whose members were over sixty-five, now saw an influx of younger activists. One of them was Susan Bernofsky, a literary translator who was teaching at Queens College in early 2012 when Joan Scott first circulated her petition (and now teaches at Columbia University's School of the Arts). Though Bernofsky had signed the petition, she had largely stayed on the margins in the months that followed. But an e-mail appeal that David Levering Lewis had dispatched before Assemblyman Kellner's hearing—an event he called "one last meaningful opportunity to prevent a cultural atrocity"—drew her in.

Bernofsky, who has translated more than twenty books from German to English (including Kafka's *The Metamorphosis*), was active in the PEN American Center. In February

2014, she and two PEN colleagues were invited to tour the empty stacks at 42nd Street. "I saw not a trace of rust on the sturdy and elegant Carnegie steel stacks," Bernofsky wrote in a blog post the next day. "A sprinkler system snaked along the ceiling, accompanied by vents for the HVAC system." When Bernofsky tried to photograph the stacks, NYPL Vice President Ken Weine, who oversees communications and marketing, forbade her:

> Weine referred me to the NYPL's "policy" prohibiting photography in the library's "non-public spaces." When I asked where I could find a record of that policy, it quickly became clear there wasn't one. I guess NYPL leadership is afraid that if enough people see actual images of the stacks in their current state—they give an impression simultaneously of vastness and solidity—they might have too many questions about why in the world the library is proposing to tear them down.

To the ranks of the CSNYPL, Bernofsky brought a facility for blogging, a busy Twitter account, and connections to the higher echelons of Manhattan's literary and publishing universe.

Another younger person who made his way to the CSNYPL in 2013 was Matthew Zadrozny. A high school dropout who graduated from the University of Pennsylvania, Zadrozny went on to earn a master's degree in computational linguistics from the University of Edinburgh. He joined the campaign in June 2013, after someone from the CSNYPL gave him a leaflet. In a blog post shortly thereafter, Zadrozny observed: "While I rarely request books from the stacks . . . this project still troubles me." Soon he himself would be leafletting in front of the Library.

L. A. Kauffman, a virtuoso organizer and activist based in Fort Greene, Brooklyn, was another newcomer. In the late 1990s, Kauffman had played a pivotal role in the rescue and preservation of nearly one hundred community gardens in New York City. To highlight the value of those spaces, she and a handful of others staged one of the most intrepid protest actions New York had seen in decades: the release of 10,000 crickets during an auction of garden lots at Police Headquarters on July 20, 1998. (Kauffman purchased the crickets on the Internet, stored them in her Midtown apartment, and, with nine other well-dressed activists, smuggled them past security in special envelopes.) The release of the crickets, the *Times* reported the next day, led to "bedlam" at the auction.

Kauffman, who had largely retreated from activism to raise two young children, was incensed to learn in March 2013 that the Brooklyn Public Library (which is separate from the NYPL) was planning to sell, to real-estate developers, a branch library on Pacific Street between tony Park Slope and gentrifying downtown Brooklyn. It was a marvelous old Carnegie building erected in 1904, and her daughter's Girl Scout troop held regular meetings in the arched-ceiling room on the second floor.

The children were upset about the prospect of losing their room, and Kauffman quickly arranged for the scouts to meet with local elected officials and to appear in a video highlighting the vitality of the library—efforts that resulted in a sympathetic article in *The New York Daily News*. Kauffman also brokered a meeting between a distinguished old friend—the writer Jonathan Lethem, who had used the Pacific Street Library as a child—and the leadership of the Brooklyn Public Library. Many others contested the sale of the 1904 building, and officials soon retreated from their plan to sell it.

By fall of 2013, Kauffman was ready to enlist in the NYPL wrangle; she had been talking to her old friend Zack Winestine, whom she had met during the anti-globalization movement in the late 1990s. But she had concerns about the CSNYPL: she felt its members lacked the expertise and digital savvy to vanquish the mighty NYPL and the Parkside Group. In her view, the critics were too focused on the fate of the old stacks and the needs of researchers and writers, and not vocal enough about the sale of a significant public asset—the Mid-Manhattan Library.

Kauffman and a friend, Lisa Guido, decided to establish their own group, which they called the Library Lovers League; it would be edgier and more theatrical than the CSNYPL. "It was never intended to be a standard organization, with a membership and formal meetings," says Kauffman. "It was an informal network of activists who came together to create a sustained social media presence, organize some high-profile street actions, and influence the overall strategy and framing of the library campaign." By late November 2013, Kauffman and Guido had fashioned a two-pronged strategy: "to create a steadily worsening public relations disaster for NYPL," and to "reach out to as many key players as possible in the progressive coalition that had elected Bill de Blasio."

On December 16, 2013, the Library Lovers League organized a "Books Not Billionaires Flash Mob to Save NYPL," in which they encouraged participants to show up on the steps of the 42nd Street Library dressed as real-estate moguls and as their favorite books. It was a frigid afternoon, and the turnout was modest, but the sight of children dressed as Harry Potter books—and adults outlandishly outfitted in yachting attire—caught the attention of the press, and the event was covered by newspapers and commercial news radio stations.

De Blasio's triumph elated the activists, who had worked for almost two years to halt the plan. His victory must have worried Marx and his team, but they weren't ready to yield. The NYPL embarked on its own strategy, which combined mobilization of the public with old-fashioned backroom deal-making.

In order to proceed with the demolition of the stacks, the NYPL needed prior approval from state historic preservation officials in Albany, with whom Marx had held a number of private meetings in 2013. Five weeks after de Blasio was elected, Marx got the authorization he needed from state officials, who conducted all their proceedings behind closed doors. Albany insisted on one stipulation: the corpse had to be properly dressed for burial. Before proceeding with demolition of the stacks, the NYPL was instructed to hire an archaeologist or historian to document, via photography and archival evidence, the totality and grandeur of Carrère and Hastings's iron-and-steel hive.

At the same time, Marx made one last attempt to sway the newly elected mayor and City Council; his weapon was the NYPL's huge database of e-mail addresses. In 2010, the Library had successfully used it to generate 100,000 petition letters to elected officials, demanding higher levels of funding. On January 16, 2014, the NYPL dispatched a new petition letter titled: "Remind City leaders that you love NYPL." Embedded in the fine print, however, was language supporting Foster's renovation. The CSNYPL and the Library Lovers League instantly launched a social media campaign to discredit the mass mailing, and Kimmelman rebuked the NYPL on Twitter, calling the petition letter "unbecoming" and "dodgy."

The campaign had entered the fast-moving realm of social media. On February 24, 2014, Matthew Zadrozny sent a loud e-mail to the CSNYPL listserv titled: "CSNYPL will get 6 million eyeballs tomorrow at 10:30 am/please be ready with Facebook comments!!!" For many people on the listserv, this was a puzzling message; they didn't use social media and didn't know what he was talking about. But luck had intervened: minutes earlier, Zadrozny had been standing in front of the Library, eating chicken from a camping pot and gazing pensively out onto 42nd Street, when he was approached by a digital-age luminary: Brandon Stanton, who runs the enormously popular photoblog *Humans of New York*.

Stanton asked to take Zadrozny's picture. "*You want to photograph me eating chicken?*" Zadrozny replied. "Yep," said Stanton. They struck a deal. "If I let you," said Zadrozny, "I need you to help me deliver a message." This was the message he delivered in the caption:

> It's my favorite place in the world. As many people know, the main reading room of this library is supported by seven floors of books, which contain one of the greatest research collections in the world. Recently, the library administration has decided to rip out this collection, send the books to New Jersey, and use the space for a lending library. As part of the consolidation, they are going to close down the Mid-Manhattan Library branch as well as the Science, Industry and Business Library. When everything is finished, one of the greatest research libraries in the world will become a glorified internet café. Now read that back to me.

The next morning, Zadrozny sent a follow-up message to the CSNYPL listserv, which included a link to the *HONY* photo and caption. That message was titled: "here it is—right on time."

The photo flew across social media. Within twenty-four hours, it had been shared 47,000 times and received 215,000 likes, making it one of the most viral pictures to be published by *HONY*. Ten thousand comments, most of them severely critical of the NYPL—"I support stopping this madness 1000%," wrote one person—were posted on *HONY*'s Facebook page. (Zadrozny also received scores of marriage proposals. "I don't know who you are," one admirer wrote, "but I will find you and I will marry you.") The activists seized a golden opportunity: Winestine, Kauffman, and Guido remained at their computers for forty-eight hours, posting hundreds of comments to *HONY*'s Facebook page and steering concerned readers to the CSNYPL's online petition to Mayor de Blasio.

For Zadrozny, the *HONY* affair amounted to a surreal experience. "I had no idea who Brandon Stanton was," he told me months later. "But I knew about *Humans of New York*, I liked the site, and I knew it was big. Still, I was shocked to find the site had three million likes."

Using new media tools, Stanton and Zadrozny delivered a devastating traditionalist critique to a mainstream audience. Zadrozny was soon profiled on *The Atlantic*'s website, and Caleb Crain would observe that the *HONY* picture made him "the closest thing the campaign got to a Jackie Onassis," whose efforts helped to save Grand Central Terminal in 1975. The fate of the NYPL was no longer just an obsession for bookworms, scholars, librarians, historic preservationists, and those in the know—the cause had gone mainstream.

At the same time, prominent literary figures were growing more vocal. Writers had largely remained silent since Joan Scott's petition in early 2012, but there were a few exceptions. At a May 2013 Q&A session at BookExpo America, the publishing industry's biggest trade show, Malcolm Gladwell offered a blunt critique of the NYPL's expansion: "Every time I turn around, there's some new extravagant renovation going on in the main [NYPL] building. Why?" He added, tongue firmly in cheek, "Luxury condos would look wonderful there."

By early 2014, more writers were ready to get involved, and they allowed the CSNYPL and the Library Lovers League to roll out written statements every few days. Some were elegiac. "To destroy a library is to destroy the dream of civilization," wrote Junot Díaz. "To destroy the NY Public Library is to destroy our sixth and best borough; that beautiful corner of New York City where all are welcome and all are equals, and where many of us were first brought to the light." Other statements were acidic. "Whatever its rationale, advertised or secretly savored," E. L. Doctorow wrote, "the Central Library Plan is an act of such manic mutilation as to constitute a death wish for the 42nd Street Research Library."

Artists, too, were reaching for their pens. In late March 2014, Scott asked Art Spiegelman, the Pulitzer Prize–winning author of *Maus*, for a brief statement of support. Instead, Spiegelman sent her a stark drawing in which a ferocious leopard streaked with dollar signs is poised triumphantly on the back of one of the NYPL lions, Patience, who

DON'T GUT OUR LIONS

has collapsed in sorrow, and who appears to be holding back tears; the lion's torso bears a grisly, mortal wound. In its left paw, the leopard brandishes a book that is oozing blood; another battered volume extrudes from the predator's razor-edged teeth. Spiegelman's image, which bore a stylistic resemblance to the political art of the 1930s, and which initially appeared on the CSNYPL website, had a pithy caption: "DON'T GUT OUR LIONS."

Staff members came to suspect that Marx was ambivalent about fundamental aspects of the CLP: during internal meetings, he seemed more animated about the Library's social service mission—literacy classes, after-school programs—than about the urgency of dismantling historic book stacks. Some employees wondered if Marx's zealous public advocacy for the CLP flowed from his desire to satisfy the man he referred to as "the second most important donor in the Library's history"—Stephen A. Schwarzman.

One staff member used a Vietnam-era analogy to illustrate the situation in which he believed Marx found himself: "Tony had to literally destroy the 42nd Street Library in order to save it." To "save" the NYPL meant pleasing Schwarzman: staff members knew that his $100 million gift was not delivered in one installment, but dispersed at regular intervals over five years, giving him wide, ongoing influence in the trustee room.

Schwarzman did not return my phone calls, but I had a chance to speak with him after the trustees concluded their meeting of March 12, 2014, and retreated to their regular cocktail hour. Had he personally lobbied Mayor Bloomberg for the $150 million that was allocated to the NYPL in 2011? "I know Mike," Schwarzman replied, "but I didn't have to. His sister was on the board." Indeed: Mayor Bloomberg's representative to the NYPL's board of trustees was his sister, Marjorie Tiven.

Was the $9 million paid to Norman Foster part of his $100 million gift to the Library? Schwarzman, a man famously enamored of micromanagement, looked down at his shoes and murmured: "I'm not sure how the Library is spending my money."

At this point, an NYPL communications official intervened to halt the conversation. But Schwarzman had something else to say: "Don't be an adversary. The renovation will be great."

But the renovation was in trouble. In late March 2014, Gale Brewer, the newly elected Manhattan Borough President, distributed a letter she had just written to Marx, summarizing a recent summit in his office. "Dear Dr. Marx: Thank you so much for the informative meeting," Brewer's letter began. "I am especially pleased that your team continues to take the time to get this project right." The bad news was delivered in paragraph four: "I again reiterate my belief that the sale of the Mid-Manhattan branch would be an unacceptable solution." For Marx, this was a major roadblock, because the money for Foster's renovation depended in significant part on the sale of the Mid-Manhattan Library, and because he couldn't easily defy the Manhattan Borough President. "Everyone hated the plan," Brewer told me in December 2014, when I asked her how she got involved in the controversy.

Pressure was building on de Blasio: Winestine had organized an e-mail campaign that resulted in six thousand e-mails sent to City Hall, urging the mayor to block the CLP. The critics drew attention to a pivotal date: the upcoming deadline for the City budget, which had to be approved by the mayor, and which still contained $150 million in NYPL capital funds allocated by Bloomberg. On February 27, 2014, Pogrebin had published a piece in the *Times* titled "Library Renovation Plan Awaits Word from de Blasio," in which she wrote: "For the time being, Mr. de Blasio has let stand the $150 million in capital funds . . . but the cost analysis that he called for last summer has yet to be completed."

Tension was also building inside the trustee room. A staff member walking past the room in February 2014 heard a commotion inside: a male voice bellowing, "*You are destroying the Library!*" Moreover, at least one distinguished trustee had, at some point in 2013, shifted his position and now agreed with the critics on a fundamental point.

In a letter to me on November 21, 2014, Robert Darnton wrote: "I thought it would be preferable to leave the main building alone and to apply the $150 million to the rebuilding of the Mid-Manhattan branch; but apparently Mayor Bloomberg refused to let the funds be used for anything other than remodeling the interior of the main building." It seems that for Bloomberg, it was all or nothing.

L. A. Kauffman and others, including the veteran activist Leslie Cagan, were busy organizing people who were close to Mayor de Blasio. On April 8, a letter signed by Gloria Steinem, Susan Sarandon, and the Rev. Al Sharpton, as well as labor leaders in de Blasio's inner circle, was hand-delivered to City Hall. It began: "Dear Mayor de Blasio: We are writing to urge you to save the New York Public Library from its trustees' misguided plan." The letter continued: "Taking money from branch libraries to subsidize the NYPL's real-estate plans will hurt students, seniors, immigrants, job-seekers: the millions of New Yorkers from all walks of life who rely on this public commons."

Rumors were spreading, and they pointed in one direction: the CLP was in the grave. In late April, Carolyn McIntyre of Citizens Defending Libraries called the office of a City Council member to request a meeting about the CLP. The receptionist got confused and thought McIntyre was an NYPL official, and let drop the fact that the Foster renovation had been canceled.

At 1:15 p.m. on May 7, hours before the mayor was to announce his final budget, a headline flashed across the homepage of the *Times* website: "NYPL Scraps Plan to Revamp Flagship." "In a striking about-face," Pogrebin wrote, "the New York Public Library has abandoned its much-disputed renovation plan." She reported that Marx had recently met with de Blasio, and she quoted a City Hall press official who said the administration was "pleased" by the Library's sudden shift in its plan.

Pogrebin's online scoop caught Marx by surprise: twenty-one minutes later, he sent an e-mail to his staff: "Dear colleagues: The *Times* has posted an article reporting that the Library is exploring an evolution of our plans . . . No final decisions have been reached." After receiving that e-mail from a staff member, I immediately sought comment from the mayor's press secretary, Phil Walzak, who was tight-lipped. Four hours later, an NYPL press release confirmed Pogrebin's story: the stacks would be spared, and the Mid-Manhattan Library would be retained and renovated.

Though Mayor de Blasio declined to be interviewed for this book, and his press secretary did not respond to inquiries, former assemblyman Micah Kellner suggests that de Blasio was key to the CLP's downfall: "As I understood it, the de Blasio administration told the NYPL's leadership: either drop the CLP that destroys the stacks and sells Mid-Manhattan, or he would remove the $150 million from his capital budget." (De Blasio's press office will not reveal the fate of the $150 million in capital funds destined for the NYPL.)

The reaction was ecstatic. "Phew!" tweeted Simon & Schuster's official account. "When they finished doing their due diligence I think they recognized that there was another way, a better way," David Nasaw told the *Times*. "For the people of this city and for the library it's a great victory." On

Twitter, Michael Kimmelman wrote: "Thrilled NYPL had the vision+courage to change course. Ada Louise would be happy."

When it was over, Marx was interviewed by the PBS program *Metrofocus*. His dark hair had gone gray; the NYPL wars had aged him. The CLP, he said mournfully, was "an ingenious plan, a controversial plan." He pledged that the renovated Mid-Manhattan Library will be "the most fantastic branch library you've ever seen." In another interview, on WNYC radio, he admitted: "A lot of the criticism we heard turned out to be correct."

Marx's allies could only shake their heads. The *Times* reported the CLP's demise on its front page, and followed up with an editorial titled "Common Sense at the Library." By contrast, a *Daily News* editorial lamented: "Remember the beautiful, light-filled renderings commissioned, for $9 million, from famed British architect Sir Norman Foster? Remember how fantastic it was all going to be, as indefatigably touted by NYPL boss Tony Marx?" The editorial blamed "fatally short sighted planning by the library that failed to take rising costs into account."

Rising costs were indeed an issue: on June 1, 2014, Pogrebin reported in the *Times* that the NYPL's own independent audit had shown that the Foster renovation would have cost more than $500 million, not $300 million. When the trustees on the executive committee voted to officially terminate the plan, only one person abstained: Stephen A. Schwarzman.

•

But the finale proved bittersweet for the critics. On May 9, 2014, two days after the big announcement, *The Wall Street Journal* reported that the stacks at 42nd Street would remain empty. "Stacks without books," David Levering Lewis told the *Journal*. "Isn't this pretty Kafka-esque?" "The empty stacks," Stanley Katz told me, "are the lasting image of the controversy . . . 'Take that, wise guys,' is what I fear they are saying to us." For Charles Warren, the empty hive raises the possibility of a CLP II, in which the trustees bide their time and push for demolition somewhere down the road. "As long as the stacks are empty," he says, "they are in jeopardy." In a postmortem for the *New Yorker*'s website, Caleb Crain wrote: "A few years ago, the library spent fifty million dollars restoring its façade. It's painful to think that the money can't be found to repair its heart."

The critics saved the Mid-Manhattan Library, and prevented the demolition of the stacks. But the fate of the three million books stored there remains unclear. Many of those books are in the hands of a private storage company, and are likely to end up in the storage facility under Bryant Park, which Marx said in May 2014 he will finally renovate (the work has not yet started); many have gone to offsite storage in Princeton; and many seem to have gone missing when the stacks were emptied. The result is chaos and misery for researchers. On January 15, 2015, Paula Glatzer, the scholar and CSNYPL activist, wrote a letter to Marx:

> Sadly, I have had to tell my colleagues that the NYPL is over . . . for now. Many of the books are off-site. Many are mislabelled as on-site when they're off. Books can take many days to be delivered, and email communication is spotty. Other books have been lost . . . or discarded. I requested a series. It couldn't be found. I said it was hard to lose 21 volumes. A librarian overheard me and offered to look. He later e-mailed: All 21 volumes were indeed missing.

Another lasting image of the controversy is the fifty-story glass tower on the site of the old Donnell Library, which was finally demolished in 2011. It contains sixty apartments (including the penthouse that was marketed for $60 million and remains unsold), and the new Baccarat Hotel, which has 114 guestrooms, the cheapest of which is $900. In February 2015, a Chinese insurance company bought the hotel for $230 million, creating a windfall for Starwood Capital Group and Tribeca Associates, which had taken over the contract from Orient-Express. *The Wall Street Journal* called it "the most highly valued hotel in the U.S."

And the new branch library at the base of the tower? It has yet to be constructed. It will cost the NYPL $21 million, or one-third of the $59 million the Library received for the property.

The Science, Industry and Business Library on 34th Street will be sold. NYPL officials say the Mid-Manhattan Library will be fully renovated by 2020.

8

"The Wrong Plan"

It was a brawl about democracy, architecture, and, crucially, the role of books in the digital age. In the 1890s, the 42nd Street Library was designed to collect and organize the world's essential written materials; it was a highly fruitful experiment. In 1942, the NYPL's annual report included a complete list of items requested in a single hour on a single day—November 30, 1942, from 2:30 to 3:30 p.m., during which 126 readers submitted 231 call slips. The report noted:

> Forty-six volumes of general periodicals were called for. Three readers wanted recent volumes of *Life*; another called for *Vogue*, *Harper's Bazaar*, and the *Ladies' Home Journal*. In the broad field of literature Emerson's *Conduct of Life*, and Franklin's *Sayings of Poor Richard* were among the titles. Three volumes of modern Icelandic fiction and two novels by Ignazio

> Silone were asked for . . . Readers interested in crime and detection asked for August Mencken's *By the Neck: A Book of Hangings*, and for two books by the famous Pinkerton. There was a request for the Census of 1931 for Trinidad and Tobago, and another for an address delivered . . . by the governor general of French Equatorial Africa.

Moreover:

> Sixteen books classified as Philosophy and Religion were given out. This group included: Uspenski's *A New Model of the Universe*; Foxe's *Book of Martyrs*; and *De Atheniensium pompis sacris*, Berlin, 1900, by Pfuhl. In the field of philology . . . one reader received a Hungarian grammar, and another, *Chinese Made Easy*. Three books on legerdemain by Horace Goldin, one with the title, *It's Fun to Be Fooled*, and *Kellar's Wonder Book* were consulted by an aspiring young magician. The following biographies were asked for: Daniel C. Roper's *Fifty Years of Public Life*, Frank Wilstach's *Wild Bill Hickok*, and the Stackpole edition of Adolf Hitler's *Mein Kampf*.

Today, the NYPL's users still read books on Emerson, Franklin, public life, the Chinese language, and Nazi Germany. But many are reading them on iPhones, Kindles, and tablets. The use of paper materials has fallen in the Library's research division. Ten years ago, on the elegant wooden benches in the Rose Reading Room, it was not unusual for eight or nine people to be waiting for materials from the stacks. Today, two or three people occupy those benches. The elegant periodicals room, refurbished in the 1980s, has turned into a ghost town, as bored clerks tend to stacks of unread newspapers, magazines, and journals. The microfilm room, too, has seen a decline in users, though it is far from deserted.

None of this happened overnight: in his *New Yorker* profile of Vartan Gregorian, Philip Hamburger interviewed one of his deputies, Joan Dunlop, who remarked: "I have many worries about the Library. I am not certain it is being used the way it once was, what with the great university libraries all over the city."

Indeed, there are fewer professors at 42nd Street these days: many academics download scholarly material to their home computers with passwords linked to their own campus libraries. But the occupants of the Rose Reading Room remain as diverse as ever: students researching term papers with the aid of the NYPL's expensive databases; aspiring novelists hunched over labyrinthine texts by David Foster Wallace, Thomas Pynchon, and William H. Gass; scholars from Latin America, Asia, and Africa; freelance scribes, researchers, and graphic designers; the world-weary old men, dressed in outmoded suits; the eccentrics of every variety; the homeless and near-homeless; the people seeking refuge from the rain.

This isn't the place for a colloquy about the library in the digital age, in part because the NYPL is distinct from the nation's best public library systems. The institution, until very recently, was singular—a world-class public research library on par with the Library of Congress, the Harvard library system, the British Library, and the Bibliothèque nationale in Paris.

At a public event in 2012, Sam Roberts—an old-school reporter for the *Times*, an authority on New York City, and a man known for his equanimity—referred to the CLP as "radical." He was right, of course, but the plan's radicalism was closely linked to the techno-utopian moment in which it was born: by the time it was set in motion, Google was digitizing millions of books (including many out-of-copyright books from the NYPL's own collection) in a highly ambitious, essentially for-profit venture. A veteran NYPL staff member observes: "Planning for the CLP assumed that Google would be able to deliver in-copyright books online so on-site physical collections could be removed."

The NYPL's trustees rushed to embrace the digital future heralded by Google Books. In June 2008, a year after the approval of the CLP, individuals inside the NYPL (their identity is unknown) sounded an alarm about potential damage to the Library's research capacity. That warning was no more than a hiccup in the trustee-meeting minutes of June 4, 2008, which note: "Some trustees and staff members have expressed concern over the role of the research libraries in the Library's future plans, and [the chairman] suggested that a discussion take place on this topic later in the meeting." The "point of departure" for that discussion was an essay, "The Library in the New Age," that Robert Darnton had published a few days earlier in *The New York Review of Books.*

It is one of Darnton's most radiant essays, one that touches on his tour of duty in 1959 as a police reporter in Newark, New Jersey (an experience right out of *The Front Page*), and his latest archival adventures ("I recently discovered an extraordinary libertine novel, *Les Bohémiens*, by an unknown author, the marquis de Pelleport, who wrote it in the Bastille at the same time that the marquis de Sade was writing his novels in a nearby cell"). But the core of Darnton's essay is a nuanced discussion about paper books and e-books, and their uneasy coexistence.

"I speak as a Google enthusiast," Darnton wrote, "although I worry about its monopolistic tendencies." He proceeded to ask pointed questions about Google's scheme for digitizing books: "How can Google keep up with current production while at the same time digitizing all the books accumulated over the centuries? Better to increase the acquisitions of our research libraries than to trust Google to preserve future books for the benefit of future generations."

One shouldn't assume, he wrote, that Google's copies will last: "Bits become degraded over time. Documents may get lost in cyberspace, owing to the obsolescence of the medium in which they are encoded. Hardware and software become extinct at a distressing rate. Unless the vexatious problem of digital preservation is solved, all texts 'born digital' belong to an endangered species."

Darnton's reverence for the book as a physical object accounted for the essay's most evocative passage:

> When I read an old book, I hold its pages up to the light and often find among the fibers of the paper little circles made by drops from the hand of the vatman as he made the sheet—or bits of shirts and petticoats that failed to be ground up adequately during the preparation of the pulp. I once found a fingerprint of a pressman enclosed in the binding of an eighteenth-century *Encyclopédie*—testimony to tricks in the trade of printers, who sometimes spread too much ink on the type in order to make it easier to get an impression by pulling the bar of the press.

Darnton's conclusion was directed at research libraries in general: "Shore up the library. Stock it with printed matter." What did NYPL trustees say in their discussion of Darnton's essay? The minutes don't tell us, and Darnton was not in the room to hear it. But the trustees were clearly moving in the other direction, toward a library that would keep most of its books in New Jersey. Would Darnton's essay have made a difference if it had appeared a year before the CLP was ratified? Almost certainly not: business leaders ruled the NYPL's board, and Darnton was just a scholar, albeit the most reputable one on the board.

"The digital transition allowed the Library for the first time to consider shifting away from research," says Charles Petersen of *n+1*. "Before, say, 2000, its sunk-costs in the research library were so high that the institution couldn't ever really consider doing anything else: it had to stay the course on the path set for it in the 1910s. Digital changed all that. Now the trustees could decide whether they really wanted to put all this money into a research library." Concludes Petersen: "I strongly believe no radical change was *necessary* to bring the Library into the twenty-first century."

In 2011, three years after Darnton published that essay, a federal judge rejected a carefully constructed settlement regarding Google's scanning of books, dashing the hopes of techno-utopians; the NYPL's trustees, like others, had greatly underestimated the complexities of copyright law. In the wake of that legal decision, most of the books in the NYPL's vast collection are *not* electronically accessible. By and large, only books published *before* 1923 can be read in full-text digital format. This state of affairs is likely to continue with regard to books and copyright, unless Congress takes decisive action.

All of which points to the wisdom of Caleb Crain's observation in his 2012 blog post, "Build More Deliberately": "Why not wait to reconceive the library until we know a little more about how scholars will use books and e-books in the digital age?"

Marx eventually reached the same conclusion. In a May 2014 radio interview, he admitted: "The plan to move the majority of books offsite was the wrong plan. That was pretty clear pretty early on."

In the 1890s, the NYPL's founding trustees were prominent men like Philip Schuyler, the great-grandson of Alexander Hamilton; William Allen Butler, whose father had been Andrew Jackson's Secretary of War; and Lewis Ledyard, J. P. Morgan's lawyer and Edith Wharton's cousin. Nearly all the trustees contributed significant amounts of money to the new Library. In her 1972 history of the NYPL, Phyllis Dain wrote that the founding board "was largely unrepresentative of those whom the library was expected to serve . . . The typical trustee was a man past his prime." And yet those men understood the NYPL's mission, and were prudent in their stewardship of the institution.

That model of elite governance was far from perfect, but it worked reasonably well until the 1960s and '70s, when funding from the city, the state, and the federal government began to wither. Brooke Astor and Vartan Gregorian filled the leadership void in the 1980s; they embodied a fine old tradition in philanthropy: the wealthy, golden-hearted donor and the supremely capable administrator working together on behalf of the public good.

The LeClerc years, though, saw a shift in the delicate equilibrium between NYPL executives, wealthy trustees, and in-house librarians. Gregorian had many affluent people on his board, but he was in charge, and he valued the opinions of his staff. LeClerc, by contrast, gave his trustees too much freedom: business leaders were allowed to apply top-down corporate solutions to the NYPL's complex problems. A world-famous cultural institution, whose public mission entailed the free dissemination of information, was now in the hands of trustees so unaccountable they would not even give their résumés to journalists.

A democratic thread that runs through the NYPL's history was thereby severed. In 1897, after John Shaw Billings had created his design for the 42nd Street Library, he reached out to leading architects and experts for alternative schemes and floor plans that would challenge his own conception of what the building should be. In his 1923 history of the NYPL, Harry Lydenberg noted: "This was very characteristic of Dr. Billings' openmindedness."

After Billings had collected a number of designs from his open competition, he gave them to the newspapers, which, in Lydenberg's words, "eagerly commented on them as news." Billings also sent the terms of the competition to the nation's top librarians, to whom he posed questions: "Is it well to place the large public reading room or reading rooms on the upper floor (as shown in the diagrams), with access by elevators, or is it better to put these rooms on a lower floor?" Because of Billings, the plans for the 42nd Street Library were debated at the general meeting of the American Library Association in 1897.

These days, library democracy is hardly moribund in the United States. A striking counterpoint to the NYPL is the

Seattle Public Library, which remade its system in the 1990s in a remarkably transparent process. According to the New School's Shannon Mattern, who writes on libraries, Seattle City Librarian Deborah Jacobs held more than one hundred meetings with the public to solicit a wide range of input. LeClerc and Marx chose another path: between 2006 and 2014, the NYPL did not sponsor a single public meeting about the CLP.

At an early stage in the NYPL wars, activists were dismayed to realize the extent to which Library officials were unaccountable. In March 2009, two high-ranking NYPL executives held a tension-filled meeting with Manhattan's Community Board 5, whose members were worried about the fate of the nearby Donnell. In a letter to LeClerc, the chairman of CB5, David Siesko, wrote: "It was also pointed out that the NYPL is not a government agency and is not therefore obligated to consult with the public."

Nor did the NYPL feel compelled, in 2012, to share information with the country's most eminent architecture critic. On May 14, 2014, Eric Gibson, who edits *The Wall Street Journal*'s Leisure & Arts section, published a piece in the *Journal* titled "The Huxtable New York Public Library: In Gratitude to the Woman Who Thwarted a Misguided Renovation Plan." Gibson, who was Huxtable's editor, wrote: "It's worth noting that Ms. Huxtable determinedly pursued the story over several months in the teeth of escalating illness and Nixonian levels of stonewalling by library officials. A few days after her article appeared, she entered the hospital for the last time." Apropos of the NYPL's trustees, Gibson observed that Huxtable "helped save them from themselves."

Even some trustees see the absence of transparency as a fundamental issue. Says David Remnick, editor of *The New Yorker* and a longtime NYPL trustee: "For me, the great thing lacking from the start was genuine public involvement, public discussion. A more democratic, noisy process."

Baleful results flowed from the Library's secrecy. Spokesman Ken Weine says the NYPL spent $18 million on the CLP—a staggering expenditure for a library system that has difficulty keeping soap, toilet paper, and paper towels in the bathrooms of its eighty-eight branch libraries. The actual figure is probably much higher, but Marx and Weine won't give a detailed breakdown of the CLP's costs. It's not clear how Schwarzman's $100 million gift was dispersed, but it's likely that $9 million of it was squandered on Foster's fees.

The NYPL's penchant for secrecy was abetted by the apathy of elected officials, who, in recent decades, have seemed more interested in the Library's social service mission—English classes, programs for children and immigrants, tax information seminars—than in its research function, its decaying facilities, and its internal governance. And so the trustees were left alone to put the institution at risk. Nicole Gelinas was correct to observe in the *New York Post* that a $500 million overhaul could have resulted in the NYPL's bankruptcy.

Along with LeClerc and Marx, a core group of high-ranking trustees—Marshall Rose, Joshua Steiner, Roger Hertog (who left the board), Catherine Marron, and Neil Rudenstine—bear responsibility for a grand folly. It must be said that, as philanthropists, several of these individuals have been exceedingly generous to the NYPL: the Library's recent annual reports suggest that Marron has given at least $30 million since 2008; Rose and Steiner have each contributed at least $5 million, and probably much more.

Darnton believes that the NYPL's trustees were ill-treated in the public debate. "I never encountered anything resembling malfeasance or misconduct or bad faith in any of my dealings with the Library," Darnton wrote to me in late 2014. "The board members devote a lot of their time, not just their money, to trying to make a great library greater. Speaking as one who never spent much time with wealthy people, I must say that I learned to admire the hard work that the trustees devote to the public good. The attacks on them were unfair and wrong."

Hard-working or not, those trustees had to be saved from themselves. In its moment of crisis, the NYPL was rescued in large part by independent scholars and writers—a group that, as Annalyn Swan wrote in the Fall 2014 issue of *The Threepenny Review*, "makes its living, an often meager and idealistic one, off words and ideas, in a city where big money talks."

•

In his *New Yorker* piece, Hamburger quoted one of Vartan Gregorian's colleagues on the NYPL board: "Gregorian's dream, and long-term plan, I think, is that one day this great national treasure will be placed on a basis comparable to the Library of Congress or the Smithsonian as a national asset with a fixed annual amount." In a 2014 letter to me, Gregorian wrote: "I believed then—as I do now—that the New York Public Library is a national institution as well as a global institution, serving our nation and the world. Hence, it deserved then and deserves today federal support for its national and international role."

It remains a dream. A veteran NYPL staff member recalls hearing about a lobbying trip to Washington, D.C., in the 1990s, in the course of which his colleagues were asked by Senator Robert Byrd: *What has the New York Public Library ever done for the people of West Virginia?*

The NYPL needs government regulation. It also needs a new generation of public-spirited trustees, who fully understand the Library's founding mission, who are not enamored of corporate logic, and who have assimilated the words that Kimmelman published in the *Times* during the furor over *Kindred Spirits*: "Museums and libraries are not commercial enterprises. Growth is not necessarily good. Expansion is not always wise. Often it's the reverse. True success is measured by hard-to-quantify intangibles: the quality of research and education; the study, care and maintenance of the collections; the level of public trust."

ACKNOWLEDGMENTS

In my three and a half years covering the New York Public Library, I received substantial and indispensable assistance from a small group of devoted librarians. I directed hundreds of questions to these professionals, and they answered every one. They never let me down. They cannot be named, but they have my deepest gratitude.

The following people offered solidarity, assistance, and advice: Leonard Benardo, Robert Boynton, Peg Breen, Carl Bromley, Kelly Burdick, Chris Calhoun, Roane Carey, Holly Case, Aaron Cohen, Brent Cunningham, Naresh Fernandes, David Glenn, Ronald Grele, Don Guttenplan, Eric Hershberg, Gennady Kolker, James Marcus, Graciela Mochkof-sky, Gabriel Pasquini, Danny Postel, Thom Powers, Judy Rein, Aaron and Marya Schock, Matthew Schuerman, David Smith, Ilan Stavans, Anya Stiglitz, Steve Wasserman, Sasha Waters Freyer, Jennifer Weiss, and the staff of the Independent Budget Office of the City of New York.

For their hospitality and kindness in our initial months in Istanbul in 2014, I thank Nicole Pope, Sami Ovadya, Aygen

Aytaç, Victoria Holbrook, Suzy Hansen, Cemal Filge, Ozlem Aslan, Ayşa Wieting, Ayca Gozmen, Adila Öztürk, Yeşim and Serhat Midilli, and the staff at both the 116 Residence in Sisli and the Inn City Hotel in Nisantasi.

Special thanks to my mentor Victor S. Navasky, for his unfailing sagacity and humor, and to Katrina vanden Heuvel, who has supported my work for many years, and who gave me wide latitude to investigate the NYPL. Both of them embody the finest qualities of the journalistic profession.

Patience and Fortitude was completed with the assistance of Joan K. Davidson and her colleagues at Furthermore grants in publishing, whom I salute.

Eric Banks, Caleb Crain, and Philip Pochoda provided scrupulous critiques of the manuscript, as did Norman Oder, whose dual expertise in New York City politics and public libraries was enormously useful to me. I was lucky to have Richard Kreitner as my research assistant and Melissa Flashman as my agent. Mark Krotov was the ideal editor for this project. It was a pleasure to work with Claire Kelley, Julia Fleischaker, and Wah-Ming Chang at Melville House.

Appreciation to four close friends: Craig Werner, my mentor at UW–Madison in the late 1980s; Eyal Press, for his steady encouragement and wisdom; Adam Shatz, for holding me to high standards and for being a mensch; and John Palattella, whose blue pencil has enhanced my writing for fifteen years, and whose friendship has sustained me.

I'm deeply grateful for the unwavering love and support of my family—Joy Mazur, my mother; Alan Schlossberg, my stepfather; and Arnold and Jill Sherman.

Finally, there is Bharati Sadasivam, my first and best editor, who enriches my life every day.

NOTE ON SOURCES

This book was reported in New York City between May 2011 and July 2014. It was written in Istanbul in the second half of 2014.

Chapter 1 owes a large debt to Phyllis Dain's *The New York Public Library: A History of Its Founding and Early Years.* It was published by the NYPL in 1972, but it is a totally independent work.

Chapter 2 could not have been written without the archive of *The New York Times,* whose coverage of the NYPL in the 1950s, 1960s, and 1970s was remarkably deep and comprehensive. Long live the Sulzberger family.

Chapters 3 to 8 are based on my own reporting, some of which appeared in *The Nation.*

In early 2013, with the assistance of Robert Freeman of the Committee on Open Government in Albany, I obtained, under the Open Meetings Law, the trustee-meeting minutes of the full NYPL board. I later obtained the minutes of the board's executive committee, which is the Library's highest decision-making body. For purposes of clarity and readability, I have, for the most part, referred to these documents as simply the "trustee-meeting minutes."

Certain NYPL staff members, fearing reprisals from their supervisors, spoke to me on the condition that I not identify them by name. I have honored those requests.

INDEX

ABOUT THE AUTHOR

SCOTT SHERMAN is a contributing writer for *The Nation*. His work has appeared in *Vanity Fair*, *London Review of Books*, *The Washington Post*, *Los Angeles Times*, *Newsday*, *Dissent*, *Lingua Franca*, and other publications. Sherman's reporting on the upheaval at the New York Public Library received a 2015 New York Press Club Award for Journalism. His website is scottgsherman.com.